Fairfax County, Virginia

Will Book Abstracts
1745-1748

Ruth and Sam Sparacio

The Antient Press Collection
from

Colonial Roots
Harbeson, Delaware
2017

Colonial
Roots

Helping You Grow Your Family Tree

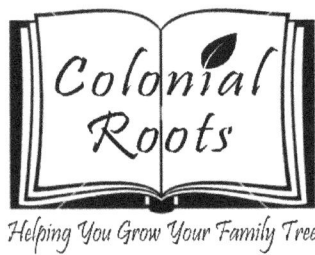

ISBN 978-1-68034-422-6

Fairfax County Will Book
1742 – 1752

Fairfax County Will Book 18ᵗʰ June 1745

-The Estate of THOMAS CARNEY, Deceased	Dr	lbs Tobacco
To paid JOHN DALTON		2563
To the Rent		730
To paid JOHN PAGAN		200
To WILLIAM PAYNE for levies		252
To 1 Clerk's Note		45
To paid WILLIAM WILLIAMS for 2 June of hhds.		160
To paid EDWARD NEAL		400
To paid ROBERT BOGGESS for levies		175
To paid JOHN PAGAN for 300 8# Nails		14
		4630
To 80# of my one Tobacco prised in one of the hhd		80
To paid JOHN DALTON in Cash		£6.11.10
To paid JARVIS the Smith for laying an Ax		0.2.0
To 600 lbs. of Tobacco Lent my father in the year 1740 a 2d		13.6.8
To 1 Gallon of Rum I found at the Appraisement		0.6.0
		£20.11.6
To clerks fee		120
To Secretary's fee		36
Per Contra		4775
By the Crop		2959
By Tobacco Received		458
By 3 levies		183
		3600
By 280 lbs. of the Tobacco I lent in the year 1740 repaid at 2d		£2.6.8
By Cash Received of JOHN SHERIDON		0.12.0
By Cash Received of JOSEPH FRY		0.1.6
By the Inventory of his Estate		3.0.2
Errors Excepted per me		83.6.2
JOHN CARNEY		£87.6.4

Fairfax County Will Book 18ᵗʰ June 1745

At a Court held for Fairfax County June 18ᵗʰ 1745.

JOHN CARNEY exhibited this account against THOMAS CARNEY's Estate on oath which is allowed by the Court and admitted to record and the Tobacco therein mentioned rated at 12s 6 per cent. Test CATESBY COCKE, Clk. Curt.

-1742 The Estate of JOHN FLOYD, Deceased	Dr	lbs. Tobacco
To Building a Tobacco house		800
To 2 Bushels Salt at 2 lbs.		42
To 1 Frying Pan		21
To 1 felt hat		8

To 2 Gallons Rum at 40	80
To 3 Appraisers fees at 30 per	90
1 To Mr. JOHN PAGAN	820
2 To RICHARD OSBORN	269
3 To GARRARD TRAMEL	40
To County and Parish Levys	37 1/2
To Secretarys Note	36
To CATESBY COCKE Clerk fees	120
To 1 Court Martial fine paid BOGGESS	<u>100</u>
	2497 1/2
Ballance due to the Estate in Tobacco	<u>5102</u>
	3008

To Packing and Priseing 1 hhd Tobacco and Roling 2 hogsheads

To the warehouse and inspecting the same	£1.0.0
To making a Coffin	0.6.0
1 To paid Mr. JOHN PAYNE	1.6.2
3 Paid GARRARD TRAMEL	0.0.9
4 To paid JOHN HARLE	1.1.1
5 To paid JAMES BURN	0.7.6
6 To paid ROBERT WARDEN	<u>0.2.0</u>
Pr. Contra	£4.3.6
By 1 years Accommodation	500
By the Crop made on the Plantation	<u>2508</u>
	3008
By Cash Received	£0.2.4
By Ballance due to G. ADAMS Administrator	<u>4.0.7</u>
By the Inventory	£4.3.6

June 15th 1745 Errors Excepted per GABRIEL ADAMS Administrator.
At a Court held for Fairfax County June 18th 1745.
GABRIEL ADAMS, Junior exhibited this account against JOHN FLOYD's Estate which is allowed by the Court and admitted to record and therein mentioned rated at 12s 6 per cent.   Test   CATESBY COCKE, Clk. Crt.

p.	<u>Fairfax County Will Book 18th June 1745</u>		
122	-THOMAS WILLIAMS's Estate	Dr	lbs Tobacco
		£.S.D	
	Paid to Mr. JOHN BROWN	6.6.0	
	Paid to Mr. JOHN CARLYLE		434
	Paid by Mr. JOHN PAGAN		160
	Paid to Mr. RICHARD BLACKBURN	0.3.0	
	Paid to DANIEL FRENCH, Senior		15
	Paid to THOMAS AWBREY	0.6.4	
	Paid to PATRICK MATHEWS in debt and cost	2.8.9	52
	Paid for Administration of THOMAS WILLIAMS Estate		120
	Paid to WILLIAM BOYLSTONE	0.10.0	80
	Paid to Mr. HUGH WEST	0.4.1 1/2	

Paid to Mr. TERRELL	0.11.0
Paid for Recording a Will	36
Paid to WILLIAM BOYLSTONE	0.15.0
Paid to Mr. TERRELL	0.2.0
Currency	11.6.2 1/2
Received of WILLIAM THOMAS one shilling and three	0.1.3
Pence on the Account of THOMAS WILLIAMS	
By the Inventory of his Estate	

At a Court held for Fairfax County June 18th 1745.
CHARLES THRIFT exhibited this account against THOMAS WILLIAMS's Estate on oath
which is allowed by the Court and admitted to record and the Tobacco therein
mentioned at 12s 6 per cent.   Test   CATSEBY COCKE, Clk. Curt.

-Know all men by these presents that We ANN BRONAUGH, JAMES JARVIS,
WILLIAM BRONAUGH & WILLIAM REARDON are held and firmly bound unto JOHN
COLVILL, Gent. first Justice in Commission of the Peace for Fairfax County for and in
behalf and to the sale use and behoof of the Justices of the said County and their
Successors in the sum of two hundred pounds sterling to be paid by the said JOHN
COLVILL his Executors, Admrs. and assigns to the which payment well and truly to be
made we bind ourselves and every of us our and every of our heirs Exrs. and Admrs.
Jointly and severally firmly by these presents sealed with our seals and dated this
16th day July 1745.
The Condition of this Obligation is such that if the above bound ANN BRONAUGH,
Administrator of all the Goods Chattels and Credits of JOHN BRONAUGH, Deceased
do make or cause to be made a true and perfect Inventory of all and singular the
Goods Chattels and Credits of the said Deceased which have or shall

p.   Fairfax County Will Book 16th July 1745
123   come to the hands possession or knowledge of the said ANN or unto the
       hands or possession of any other person or persons for her, and the same so
made do exhibit or cause to be exhibited into the County Court of Fairfax at such time
as she shall be thereto required by the said Court and the same Goods Chattels and
Credits, and all other the Goods Chattels or Credits of the said Deceased at the time
of his Death or which at any time after shall come to the hands or possession of the
said ANN, or unto the hands or possession of any other person persons for her do
well and truly Administer according to Law and further do make a just and true
account of her actings and doings therein, when the required by the said Court and
all the rest and residue of the said Good Chattels which shall be bound remaining
upon the said Administrx. account the same being first examined and allowed by the
Justices of the said Court for the time being shall deliver and pay unto such person or
persons respectively as the said Justices by their order or Judgment shall direct
pursuant to the Law in that case made and provided. And if it shall hereafter appear
that any last Will and Testament was made by the said Deceased and the Executor or
Executors therein named do exhibit he same into the said Court making request to
have it allowed and approved accordingly if the said ANN being thereunto required do
render and deliver up her Letters of Administration Approbation of such Testament

being first had and made in the said Court, Then this Obligation to be void else to remain in full force and virtue.

 Sealed and Delivered in presence of

 ANN Ann B [her mark] BRONAUGH [seal]

 JAMES x [his mark] JARVIS [seal]

 WILLIAM x [his mark] BRONAUGH [seal]

 WILLIAM x [his mark] REARDON [seal

ANN BRONAUGH, JAMES JARVIS, WILLIAM BRONAUGH & WILLIAM REARDON acknowledged this Bond in Fairfax County Court the 16th day of July 1745 to be their Act and Deed which is admitted to record. Test CATESBY COCKE, Clk. Curt.

 -Know all men by these presents that We ROBERT BOLING & ROBERT KING are held and firmly bound unto JOHN COLVILL, Gent. the first Justices in the Commission of the Peace for Fairfax County for and in behalf and to the sole use and behoof of the Justices of the said County and their Successors in the sum of one hundred pounds sterling to be paid to the said JOHN COLVILL his Executors Admrs. and assigns to the which payment well and truly to be made We bind ourselves and every of us our and every of our heirs Executors and Admrs. jointly and severally firmly by these presents sealed with our seals dated this 16th day of July 1745.

 The Condition of this Obligation is such that if the above bound ROBERT BOLING Admr. of all the Goods Chattels and Credits of CHARLES NEAL, Deceased do make execute or cause to be made a true and perfect Inventory of all and singular the Goods Chattels and Credits or the said deceased which have or shall come to the hands possession or knowledge of the said ROBERT or unto the hands or possession of any other person or persons for him and the same so

p. Fairfax County Will Book 16th July 1745

124 made do exhibit or cause to be exhibited into the County Court of Fairfax at such time as he shall be thereto required by the said Court and the same Goods Chattels and Credits and all other the Goods Chattels and Credits of the said deceased at the time of his Death or which at any time after shall come to the hands or possession of the said ROBERT or unto the hands or possession of any other person or persons for him do well and truly Administer according to Law and further do make a Just and true account of his Actings and doings therein when thereto required by the said Court and all the rest and residue of the said Goods Chattels and Credits which shall be found remaining upon the said Administrs. account, the same being first examined and allowed by the Justices of the said Court for the time being shall deliver and pay unto such person or persons respectively as the said Justices by their order or Judgment shall direct pursuant to the Law in that case made and provided and if it shall hereafter appear that any last Will and Testament was made by the said Deceased and the Executor or Executors therein named do exhibit and approved accordingly if the said ROBERT being therein required do render of such Testament being first had and made in the said Court. Then this Obligation to be void else to remain in full force and virtue.

 Sealed and delivered in the presence of

  ROBERT BOLING RB [his mark] [seal]

  ROBERT KING R [his mark] [seal]

ROBERT BOLING and ROBERT KING acknowledged this Bond in Fairfax County Court the 16th day of July 1745 to be their act and deed which is admitted to record.
Test   CATESBY COCKE, Clk. Curt.

-June 14th 1744 The Estate of PETER TURNER, Deceased		Dr
To 1 pair of Pumps in Cash		£0.6.0
To 1 yard and half of Brown linen		0.1.6
To Cash lent		0.2.0
To his Burning to 12 Gallon Rum		0.9.0
To his Coffin and Sheet		0.10.0
To his Grave digging		0.5.0
To paid ROBERT LINDSEY		0.4.1
Per Contra		£2.17.7
By Cash Received		0.2.7
By Sawing 285 foot of Plank		0.14.3
		£0.16.10
By Tobacco Received of JOHN CANADA	240 lbs Tobacco	
By Tobacco Received WILLIAM MEHONEY	100 lbs Tobacco	
	340	

p.   Fairfax County Will Book 16th July 1745
125   To 1 horse belonging to the Estate of PETER TURNER, Decest.   £2.0.0
       valued by the forementioned praisers whose names is under
       written.   ANDREW HUTCHISON
                          FRANCIS SUMMERS, THOMAS PINSON
          Errors Excepted per FIELDING TURNER
At a Court held for Fairfax County July 16th 1745.
FIELDING TURNER exhibited this account against PETER TURNER's Estate on oath which is allowed by the Court and admitted to record and the Tobacco therein mentioned rated at 10s percent.   Test   CATESBY COCKE, Clk. Crt.

       -Pursuant to an order of Fairfax Court dated May 21st 1745.
We whose names are under written being first sworn before JEREMIAH BRONAUGH, Gent. one of his Majesties Justices of the County aforesaid have appraised in money, and Inventoryed all and singular the Estate of RICHARD SLY, Deceased as was presented to our view [Vizt.]

To one gun 25s 3 shirts 12s6 1 pair of Checket Trousers 5s		£2.2.6
To 1 pair of thread stockens 3s 2 pair old yard Ditto 2/6		0.5.6
To 1 pair shoes 1 pair buckets and 1 old spun		0.5.0
To 1 Saddle and bridle 20s 2 Deer skins 14s		1.14.0
To 1 Coat and Vest 30s a parcel of old cloaths 5s	1.15.0	
To 1 belt 1s 1 box gun powder 1s		0.2.0
To 1 bottle 6d 1 ¼ Doz. mettle Buttons 6d		0.1.0
To Cash		12.3.2
June 12th 1745 JOHN FARGUSON		£18.8.2
OWEN GILMORE		
GEORGE PLATT		

At a Court held for Fairfax County July 16th 1745.
This Inventory and appraisement of the Estate of RICHARD SLY, Deceased was returned and admitted to record.   Test   CATESBY COCKE, Clk. Curt.

		Tobacco	Silver	Paper
-1744 The Estate of ROBERT WHITELY, Deceased	Dr			
To Cash paid to the Estate of THOMAS PEARSON			0.15.11	
To Cash and Tobacco paid THOMAS MORRIS		42	1.4.7	
To Paper Cash paid RICHARD WHEELER				1.0.0
To Cash paid GEORGE HAMILTON			0.16.9	
To Tobacco paid ANN MASON for Rent		1060		
To Tobacco paid the Sherif		374		
To Tobacco and Cash paid ROBERT BOGGESS		80	0.2.1	
To Tobacco paid GILBERT SIMPSON		600		

p.   Fairfax County Will Book 16th July 1745

126		Tobacco	Silver	Paper
To paper Cash paid MATHEW HOPKINS				4.18.7
To Lawyers for settleing the Estate			0.15.0	
To a Lawyers fee at the suit of STURMAN Assignee of JAMES TOMPSON, Junior			0.15.0	
To funeral expenses			2.10.0	
Pr Contra	Cr	2156	£4.19.11	£5.18.7
By the Crop of Tobacco in the year 1744		2248		
By Cash received of JOSEPH BOLING			0.1.3	
By Cash received of Capt. JOHN MINOR			0.1.3	
By Cash left at the time of the Intestates Death			0.3.11 1/2	
By Cash received of THOMAS WHITFORD			0.2.6	
By Cash received of HENRY COLLUM			0.3.0	
July 16th 1745		2248	£0.11.11 1/2	

Errors excepted per SUSANNAH TAYLOR Admrx. of ROBERT WHITELY.
At a Court held for Fairfax County July 16th 1745.
SUSANNA TAYLOR, Admrx. of ROBERT WHITELY, Deceased exhibited this account against his Estate on oath which is allowed by the Court and admitted to record.
                    Test   CATESBY COCKE, Cl. Cur.

-Pursuant to an order of Fairfax County Court, We whose names are under written being first sworn before JEREMIAH BRONAUGH, Gent. one of his Majesties Justices for the County aforesaid have appraised and Inventory's all and singular the Estate of WILLIAM WILLIAMS, Deceased as was presented our view [Vizt.]

To 1 Cow and Calf 30s 1 young stear 15s	£2.5.0
To 2 hogs 13s 1 old mare 7/6 1 old horse 7s6	1.10.0
To 1 old feather bed 50s 2 pair of pothooks and fork 5s	2.15.0
To 2 old rugs 14s 2 old candle sticks 4d	0.14.4
To 7 head of hogs 35s 1 young calf 5s	2.0.0
To 2 Tin pans 2s 1 Tin funel 8d 1 peper Box 4d	0.3.0
To 1 sifter 1s 1 search 1s3	0.2.3
To 1 narrow ax 2s6 1 small auger 1s	0.3.6

1 straw half bushel 1/6 1 cartoach box 1	0.2.6
To 1 old gun 10s 1 sword 1s 1 gun 15s	1.6.0
To 1 mans saddle 20s 1 old cash 2s 1 old bed tick 2s6	1.4.6
To a parcel of earthen ware	0.5.0
To 1 paid old blankets	0.10.0
July 13th 1745	13.1.1

WILLIAM GODFREY

WILLIAM PEAKE

JOHN FARGUSON

p.   <u>Fairfax County Will Book 17th July 1745</u>
127   At a Court Continued and held for Fairfax County July 17th 1745.
        This Inventory and appraisement of the Estate of WILLIAM WILLIAMS,
Deceased was returned and admitted to record. Test   CATSEBY COCKE, Cl. Cur.

        -Fairfax County, January the 2nd 1744. Then came DANIEL FRENCH, Gent.
and MARY SHEPARD, who made oath that about the 25th day of December last
JAMES POWER being sick made his last Will in a verbal manner, in form following.
The said POWER first desires all his Just debts be paid, and after that be so paid, that
the said DANIEL FRENCH keep the remaining part of the Goods Chattels and Credits
in his hands till his three children come of age namely MARY POWER, ANN POWER &
THOMAS POWER and divide and pay the same Equally Amongst their or their
Survivour of them. In Witness whereof the said DANIEL FRENCH and MARY SHEPARD
have set their hands and seals the date above.
I certifie that the above Mr. DANIEL FRENCH and MARY SHEPARD made oath as
above mentioned the date above before. RICHARD OSBORN
        DANIEL FRENCH [seal]   MARY x [her mark] SHEPARD [seal]
At a Court continued and held for Fairfax County July 17th 1745.
This nuncupative Will of JAMES POWER, Deceased was presented in Court by DANIEL
FRENCH, Gent. and admitted to record.   Test   CATSEBY COCKE, Cl. Cur.

        -In the name of God Amen. I EDMUND ENGLISH of Truro Parish in the County
of Fairfax being sick and weak of body, but of sound and perfect mind and memory
praise be to God for it, do think fit to make this my last Will and Testament in manner
and form following, making nuld and void and of none effect all other Will or Wills
heretofore by me made ordaining and declaring this to be my last Will and
Testament.
I give and bequeath to my sun WALTER ENGLISH all my lands in St. Mary's County
and one hhd of feathers and all my Tobacco and muney due to me in Westmoreland
County for lending of the General Court.
My Will and desire is that all the remainder of my Estate after all my Just debts be
paid to be equally devided betune my well beloved wife SARAH and my son WALTER
ENGLISH after my death.
Item I give to my Grandafters ELIZABETH and SARAH ENGLISH thirty shillings curant
muny. Nominateing and apointing my wife and sun whole and sold Executors of this
my last Will and Testament. In Witness whereof I have hereunto set my hand and
fixed my seall this Twententh day of June 1745.

7

Signed Sealed and Delivered in the presence of us
RICHARD COLEMAN   EDMUND E [his mark] ENGLISH [seal]
HENRY H [his mark] SNOW

p.   Fairfax County Will Book 20th August 1745
128   At a Court held for Fairfax County August 20th 1745.
        This last Will and Testament of EDMUND ENGLISH, Deceased was presented
In Court by SARAH ENGLISH & WALTER ENGLISH the Executors therein named who
made oath thereto according to Law and the same is proved by RICHARD COLEMAN
& HENRY SNOW Witnesses thereto and admitted to record. And on motion of the said
Executors and their performing what is usual in such cases, Certificate is granted
them for obtaining a Probate thereof in due form.   Test   CATSEBY COCKE, Cl. Cur.

        -Know all men by these presents that We SARAH ENGLISH, WALTER ENGLISH,
RICHARD COLEMAN & HENRY SNOW are held and firmly bound unto JOHN COLVILL,
Gent. the first Justice in the Commission of the Peace for Fairfax County for and in
behalf and to the sole use and behoof of the Justices of the said County and their
Successors in the sum of two hundred pounds sterling to be paid to the said JOHN
COLVILL his Executors Admrs. and assigns to the which payment well and truly to be
made We bind ourselves and every of us our and every of our heirs Executors and
Admrs. jointly and severally firmly by these presents sealed with our seals dated this
twentieth day of August 1745.
The Condition of this Obligation is such that if the above bound SARAH ENGLISH and
WALTER ENGLISH Exrs. of the last Will and Testament of EDMUND ENGLISH,
Deceased do make or cause to be made a true and perfect Inventory of all and
singular the Goods Chattels and Credits of the said Deceased which have or shall
come to the hands possession or knowledge of the said SARAH & WALTER or unto
the hands or possession of any other person persons for them, and the same so
made and do exhibit or cause to be exhibited into the County Court of Fairfax such
time as they shall be thereto required by the said Court and the same Goods Chattels
and Credits and all other the Goods Chattels and Credits of the said Deceased at the
time of his Death or which any time after shall come to the hands or possession of
the said SARAH & WALTER or unto the hands or said possession of any other person
or persons for them do well and truly Administer according to Law further do make a
Just and true account of their actings therein when thereto required by the said
Court. And also well and truly pay and deliver all the Legacies contained and
specified in the said Testament as far as the said Goods Chattels and Credits will
thereunto extend and the Law shall charge them, then this Obligation to be void and
of none effect else to remain in full force and virtue.
        Sealed and Delivered in presence of   SARAH S [her mark] ENGLISH [seal]
                                                     WALTER ENGLISH [seal]
                                                     RICHARD COLEMAN [seal]
                                                     HENRY H [his mark] SNOW [seal]

p.   Fairfax County Will Book 20th August 1745
129   At a Court held for Fairfax County August 20th 1745.

SARAH ENGLISH, WALTER ENGLISH, RICHARD COLEMAN & HENRY SNOW
acknowledged this bond to be their Act and Deed which is admitted to record.
Test   CATSEBY COCKE, Cl. Cur.

-In the name of God Amen. I RICHARD OMOHUNDRA of the County of Fairfax
being very sick and weak of body but of perfect and sound mind memory and
understanding thanks be to God for it, Make this my last Will and Testament in
manner and form following [Vizt.] first and principally I commend my soul into the
hands of Almighty God that gave it and my body to the ground there to be decently
buried at the discretion of my Executors hereafter named.
Item I give to my daughter MARY PENSON one Negro Girl named BRIDGET during her
and her husband JOSEPH PENSON's natural life, my said daughter MARY or her said
husband paying to my daughter SARAH, half what the said Negro Girl and her
Increase to go to their son RICHARD OMOHUNDRA PENSON to him and his heirs of
his body Lawfully begotten and if he should die without heir to go to the next male
child of the said MARY PENSON and for want of such male child to be equally divided
amongst all the children of the said MARY PENSON.
Item I give to my daughter ELIZABETH one Negro man named DICK to her and her
heirs of her body Lawfully begotten forever.
Item I desire that my wife ANN OMOHUNDRA may have half what the said Negro man
and Negro Girl shall make of Tobacco Corn Fodder Wheat and every thing else and
my daughter ELIZABETH the other half during the natural life of my wife ANN
OMOUNDRA and that this said Negro shall do any thing that my said wife shall want
done.
Item I desire that my wife ANN OMOHUNDRA may not be disturbed of doing anything
upon the Plantation and that she shall have the best house upon the Plantation to
her own proper use during her natural life.
Item I give to my wife ANN OMOHUNDRA one young black horse during her natural
life and after her decease to got to WILLIAM REMEY.
Item I give to my daughter ELIZABETH one young mare called Sugar.
Item I give to my daughter JANE one bay mare.
Item I give to my daughter SARAH one black mare called Frille.
Item I desire that my bay horse may be sold to the highest bidder to help pay my
debts.
Item I give to JOSEPH PENSON one three year old steer and one Iron Pott which is at
BENJAMIN REMEY and my new suit of cloaths coat wast coat and bretches he paying
GEORGE DUNBAR eighteen shillings for the making of the said cloaths and one gun.
Item I have a young stear that came of a cow called Goodluck to be raised upon the
Plantation to the age of about six years and then sold

p.   Fairfax County Will Book 20th August 1745
130   And the money to be stowed on the schooling of my daughter MARY
      PENSON's son RICHARD OMOHUNDRA PENSON when he shall be of the age
of about eleven or twelve years to be schooled as long as the money the said steers
shall be sold for will pay for.
Item I give to my daughter ELIZABETH the Plantation I now live on and the bed I now
lie on with furniture thereto belonging.

9

Item I give to my daughter JANE the bedd and bed cloaths which is in the kitchen after my wifes death the said bed and cloaths to be kept in good repair till she has it and delivered to her as good as it now is and one cow and calf after my wifes death.

Item I give to my daughter SARAH the bed and bed cloaths which lines under the bed my wife lies on after my wifes death the said bed to be then delivered to her with bed cloaths suitable and one cow and calf after my wifes death.

Item I give to my son WILLIAM OMOHUNDRA one shilling.

Item I give to WILLIAM GROVE one pair fustain britches and one pair of britches not made which is but out in my chest.

Item I give to my daughter ELIZABETH all the rest of my Personal Estate she paying to my daughter JANE fifteen pounds currant money two years after the death of my wife ANN OMOHUNDRA.

Item I leave JOSEPH PENSON and my daughter ELIZABETH OMOHUNDRA whole and sole Executors of this my last Will and Testament. In Witness whereof I have hereunto set my hands and affixed my seal this 13th day of July Anno Domini 1745.

> Signed and Sealed in the presence of us
> JACOB J [his mark] REMEY   RICHARD R [his mark] OMOHUNDRA [seal]
> SARAH S [her mark] REMEY
> WILLIAM GROVE

At a Court held for Fairfax County August 20th 1745.

This last Will and Testament of RICHARD OMOHUNDRA, Deceased was presented in Court by JOSEPH PENSON and ELIZABETH OMOHUNDRA the Executors therein named who made oath thereto according to Law, And the same is proved by JACOB REMEY & WILLIAM GROVE two of the Witnesses thereto, who made oath that they saw SARAH REMEY the other Witness thereto subscribed sign the same, And admitted to record. And on motion of the said Executors and their performing what is usual in such cases Certificate is granted them for obtaining a Probate thereof in due form.   Test   CATSEBY COCKE, Cl. Cur.

p.   Fairfax County Will Book 20th August 1745

131   -Know all men by these presents that we JOSEPH PENSON and ELIZABETH OMOHUNDRA, EDWARD WASHINGTON & PAUL TURLEY are held and firmly bound unto JOHN COLVILL, Gent. the first Justice in the Commission of the Peace for Fairfax County for and in behalf and to the sole use and behoof of the Justices of the said County and their Successors in the sum of two hundred pounds sterling to be paid to the said JOHN COLVILL his Executors and assigns to which payment well and truly to be made we bind ourselves and every of us our and every of our heirs Executors and Admrs. jointly and severally firmly by these presents sealed with our seals dated this 20th day of August 1745.

The Condition of this Obligation is such that if the above bound JOSEPH PENSON & ELIZABETH OMOHUNDRA Executors of the last Will and Testament of RICHARD OMOHUNDRA, Deceased do make or cause to be made a true and perfect Inventory of all and singular the Goods Chattels and Credits of the said Deceased which have or shall come to the hands possession or knowledge of the said JOSEPH or ELIZABETH or unto the hands or possession of any other person or persons for them and the same so made do exhibit or cause to be exhibited into the County Court of Fairfax at such time as they shall be thereto required by the said Court and the same

Goods Chattels and Credits and all other the Goods Chattels and Credits of the said Deceased at the time of his Death or which at any time after shall come to the hands or possession of the said JOSEPH & ELIZABETH or unto the hands or possession of any other person or persons for them, do well and truly administer according to Law further do make a Just and true account of their actings and doings therein when thereunto required by the said Court and also do well and truly pays Deliver all the Legacies contained and specified in the said Testament as farr as the said Goods Chattels will thereunto extend and the Law shall charge them. Then this Obligation to be void and of none effect else to remain in full force and virtue.

      Sealed and Delivered in presents of

                  JOSEPH I [his mark] PENSON [seal]

                  ELIZABETH X [her mark] OMOHUNDRA [seal]

                  EDWARD WASHINGTON [seal]

                  PAUL P [his mark] TURLEY [seal]

JOSEPH PENSON, ELIZABETH OMOHUNDRA, EDWARD WASHINGTON & PAUL TURLEY acknowledged this Bond in Fairfax County Court the 20th day of August 1745 to be their act and deed which is admitted to record. Test   CATSEBY COCKE, Clk. Curt.

-December the 28th day one thousand seven hundred and forty four. In the name of God Amen I JOHN RICHARDSON of Fairfax County in the Colony of Virginia Planter being very sick and weak but in

p.   Fairfax County Will Book 20th August 1745

132   perfect understanding and memory praised be God I do make this my last Will and Testament as followeth Inps. I leave my loveing wife all my pearsanaple Estate as long as she lives.

Item I give my daughter MARY GASKIN one shilling sterling.

Item I leave my sons DAVID RICHARDSON & AMOSS RICHARDSON my personaple Estate after their mother's Deceased ealkly to be devided between them.

Item and lastly I do appoint my wife and my son DAVID RICHARDSON hole and sole Executors of this my last will and Testament revoking all others Will formly be meade as Witness my hand and seal.

      Witness   JOHN RICHARDSON [seal]

      THOMAS AWBREY, JOHN GORDON

      RICHARD ROBERTS, OWEN O [his mark] McGAR

At a Court held for Fairfax County August 20th 1745.

This last Will and Testament of JOHN RICHARDSON, Deceased was presented in Court by DAVID RICHARDSON one of the Executors therein named who made oath thereto according to Law and the same is proved by THOMAS AWBREY & JOHN GORDON who declared they saw the other Witnesses thereto subscribed sign the same and admitted to record. And CATHERINE RICHARDSON having relinquished her Executorship in such cases Certificate is granted her for obtaining a probate thereof in due form.   Test   CATSEBY COCKE, Clk. Curt.

-Know all men by these presents that we DAVID RICHARDSON, THOMAS AWBREY & JOHN GORDON are held and firmly bound into JOHN COLVILL, Gent. the first Justice in the Commission of the Peace for Fairfax County for and in behalf and to the sole use and behoof of the Justices of the said County and their successors in the sum of two hundred pounds sterling to be paid to the said JOHN COLVILL his Executors Admrs. and assigns To the which payment well and truly to be made We bind ourselves and every of us our and every of our heirs with our seals dated this 20th day of August 1745.

The Condition of this Obligation is such that if the above bound DAVID RICHARDSON Executor of the last Will and Testament of JOHN RICHARDSON, Deceased do make or cause to be made a

p.   Fairfax County Will Book 20th August 1745
133   true and perfect Inventory of all and singular the Goods Chattels and Credits
       of the said Deceased which have or shall come to the hands possession or
knowledge of the said DAVID or unto the hands or possession of any other person or persons for him and the same so made do exhibit or cause to be exhibited unto the County Court of Fairfax at such time as he shall be thereto required by the said Court and the same Goods Chattels and Credits and all other Goods Chattels and Credits of the said Deceased at the time of his death or which at any time after shall come to the hands or possession of the said DAVID or unto the said hands or possession of any other person or persons for him do well and truly administer according to Law and further do make a Just and true account of their actings and doings therein when thereunto required by the said Court and also do well and truly pay and deliver all the Legacies contained and specified in the said Testament as far as the said Goods Chattels and Credits will thereunto extend and the Law shall charge him then this obligation to be void and none effect or else to remain in full force and virtue.

Sealed and Delivered in the presence of   DAVID RICHARDSON [seal]
                                            THOMAS AWBREY [seal]
                                            JOHN GORDON [seal]

DAVID RICHARDSON, THOMAS AWBREY & JOHN GORDON acknowledged this Bond in Fairfax Court the 20th day of August 1745 to be their act and deed which is admitted to record.   Test   CATSEBY COCKE, Clk. Curt.

-Dr.   The Estate of JOHN EARPE Deceased in account with JOHN PAGAN, Admr. 1745.   Tobacco

	Currency		
To my own debt		1583	
To Two levies paid		122	
To paid MOSSES CASH his part of the Crop		559	
To paid WILLIAM EARP for taking care of the Cattle &c. when sold		50	
To paid WILLIAM GLADING for selling the Estate			0.7.6
To 200 8# nails for the Tobacco		12	
To Secretarys Fees		36	
To Clerks fees		40	
To WILLIAM EARP proven account	No. 1	310	
To WILLIAM HENRY TERRELL ditto	2		0.4.8
To THOMAS AWBREY per Judgment	3	71	2.12.0
To JAMES ROBINSON pro account	4	1356	

To Cr. HENRY TAYLOR for Mrs. WHITELY			1.5.3
Per warrant			
To GARRARD ALEXANDER proven account	5	134	
To WILLIAM RAMSAY ditto	6	89	
To MATHEW HOPKINS per Judgment	7	65	
To CATHERINE EARP proven account	8		0.10.0
To WILLIAM CARRILS proven account	9		0.2.9

P.
134

Fairfax County Will Book 20th August 1745

To Widow GUMMERSON per ditto	10	427	
To MOSES CASH proven account	11	70	0.19.81
To Trouble and charges			0.12.6 3/4
To the Cr. Side 1459 lb. Tobacco at 10s			7.5.9

1745   Cr.

By Sundreys sold JOSEPH COCKERIL		2.1.9
By ditto sold PHILIP QUILL		6.17.6
By Ditto sold RICHARD WHEELER		1.6.6
By Ditto sold JAMES ROBINSON	545	
By ditto sold PHILIP QUILL		1.2.6
By ditto sold ROBERT MILLS		2.7.0
By Ditto sold WILLIAM EARP	310	
By ditto sold CHARLES THRIFT	35	
By ditto sold JOHN MURPHY		0.5.0
May nth by 2 hhds Tobacco at Falls Warehouse		

1P n 1 Neat	930	
2	909	
2 Cash	60	
A Transfer Note	676	2575
By 1459 lbs. Tobacco charged in the debtors	}	1459

Errors Excepted per JOHN PAGAN Administrator

At a Court held for Fairfax County August 20th 1745.
JOHN PAGAN Administrator of JOHN EARP deceased exhibited the account against his Estate on oath which is allowed by the Court and admitted to record and the Tobacco therein mentioned rated at 10s percent.
                Test   CATSEBY COCKE, Clk. Curt.

-September 17th Dr. the Estate of ROBERT WHITELY deceased

	Per Contra	Credit
To cash paid Mr. HUGH WEST £0.5.1	By Cash Recd. of ROBERT DIXSON	£0.18.2
To cash paid DAVID DAVIS 0.18.2	By ditto of Col. COLVILL	0.1.3

        Errors excepted per SUSANNA TAYLOR Administrator
At a Court held for Fairfax County September 17th 1745.
SUSANNA TAYLOR Administratrix of ROBERT WHITELY deceased exhibited this account against his Estate on oath which is allowed by the Court and admitted to record.
                Test   CATSEBY COCKE, Clk. Curt.

p.   Fairfax County Will Book 17th September 1745

134   -Pursuant to an order of Fairfax County Court dated July 16th 1745. We whose
        names are under written being first sworn before JEREMIAH BRONAUGH,
Gent. one of his Majesties Justices for the County aforesaid the Estate of JOHN
BRONAUGH deceased as was presented to our view [Vizt.]

To 1 stear 40s 1 young ditto 20s	£3.0.0
To 1 cow & calf 35s 1 cow and yearling 35s	3.10.0
To young stear 10s 1 heifer 10s	1.0.0
To 1 old cow and calf 30s 15 sheep 75s	5.5.0
To 1 horse 80s 1 mare and colt 70s	7.10.0
To a parcel of earthen ware	0.7.6
To 1 gun 15s 1 stone jug 2s some shoemaking tools 5s 1 servant boy	7.2.0
To a parcel of old pewter	1.2.0
To 1 chamber pot 1s 1 saddle and bridle 10s	0.11.0
To a parcel of Coopers and Carpenters tools	0.6.6
To 1 Iron pot 1s6 1 frying pan 2s	0.3.6
To 1 Flesh fork and ladle	0.1.6
To search and sifter 1/7 1 looking glass	0.3.1
To 1 hair brush 6d 1 candlestick	0.1.0
To 1 prayer book 1s 15 lbs. Wool 7s6	0.8.6
To 8 old flag bottom'd chairs 1 chest 12s	1.0.0
To a parcel of lumber	0.4.0
To 2 tubs 2 piggins and 1 paile	0.9.0
To 1 feather bed bedstead and cord	6.0.0
To 4 cyder casks	0.19.0
To 4 deer skins 5s 15 lbs. Wool @ 7 d ½	0.14.4
To 1 pair wool cards 1 wrying sive	0.2.6
To 2 stear hides 10s 25 lbs. Shor @ 3d	0.16.3
To 2 lbs. Gun powder	0.3.0
To Cash	7.2.27
	£58.1.11

                                    WILLIAM MORE
                                    THOMAS BOSMAN
                                    JOHN FARGUSON
At a Court held for Fairfax County September 17th 1745.
This Inventory and appraisement of the Estate of JOHN BRONAUGH deceased was
returned and admitted to record.   Test   CATSEBY COCKE, Clk. Curt.

        -September the 7th 1745 the Appraisers meat in Obedience to an order of
Court to appraise the Estate RICHARD OMOHUNDRA deceased and do proceed as
followeth We whose names are ounder written.

p.   Fairfax County Will Book 17th September 1745

135 To 6 cows and calves at	£9.0.0
To 3 stears and 2 heffers at	3.10.0
To 22 ould hogs and seven piggs at	4.4.0
To 1 gun	0.10.0

To 1 beed and funeture at	2.0.0	
To 1 ould Negro Fellow at	18.0.0	
To 1 yound Negro Wentch at	27.0.0	
To 1 beed and funeture at	3.10.0	
To 1 small beed at	1.0.0	
To 1 suit of new clows at	3.0.0	
To 1 suit of britches at	0.5.0	
To 1 pair of britches at	0.3.0	
To 1 healbeard and bagnet at	0.7.0	
To 1 Chest and 7 pence in Cash at	0.5.7	
To 1 looking glass at	0.6.0	
To a parcel of ould lumber at	2.10.6	
To a parcel of ould knives and forks and 1 book at	0.6.0	
To a parcel of ould iron at	0.12.0	
To a parcel ould pewter at	0.15.0	
To a punch boals and a parcel of lumber	0.9.0	
To 3 ould iron pots 1 ould saddle and 1 ould soab at	0.15.0	
To 1 parcel of ould wooden ware at	0.7.0	
To 1 mare and 2 bells and 1 bridle at	1.17.0	
To 1 sun dial at	<u>0.1.0</u>	

WILLIAM BUCKLEY £18.13.7
FIELDING TURNER
VINCENT LEWIS

At a Court held for Fairfax County September 17th 1745.
This Inventory and appraisement of the Estate of RICHARD OMOHUNDRA deceased was returned and administered to record. Test   CATSEBY COCKE, Clk. Curt.

-Dr. The Estate of Mr. ROBERT OSBORN deceased

	Tobacco	Money
To Ballance in Legr. B for 20	45	
To 5 Barrils of Corn to JOHN KING at 70 lbs per	350	
To the midwife for laying Negro BESS	100	
To GARRARD ROBINSON	900	
To Building a barn	900	
To Building a kitchen	500	
To Mr. JOHN DALTON	8184	5.0.7
To Mr. WILLIAM PAYNE	532	
To Mr. JOHN PAGAN for ROBERT WHITELY		0.5.0
To OWEN WILLIAMS		2.0.0

p.	Fairfax County Will Book 17TH September 1745	
137	To Col. RICHARD BLACKBURN	1.5.0
	To Mr. ROBERT VAULX	0.13.10
	To JEREMIAH HAMPTON	1.1.0
	To Mr. HUGH WEST	0.19.0
	To Capt. THOMAS PEARSON	1.1.5
	To BENJAMIN SEBASTIAN for Rush	0.6.6

To Mr. HENRY THRELKELD £16.12.1 ½ Sterling and			4.14.9
To WILLIAM GRIMWOOD			0.1.6
To Capt. AUGUSTINE WASHINGTON's Estate		59	2.16.8
To ROBERT BOLING paid Mr. RAMSAY		255	
To 1 Barrel of Corn to ROBERT BOLING		70	
To Capt. JOHN MINOR for WILLIAM GARRARD		615	
To Mr. JOHN DALTON for CHARLES MASON		190	
To Clerks fee to Mr. TERRELL		259	
To 7 Gallons Rum at 6s			2.2.0
To 1 Dozen of Red Wine } funeral			1.1.0
To ½ Dozen of white ditto			0.10.0
To Mr. PAGAN on account of Froom			0.19.6
To JOHN KING			1.2.2 1/2
To ROBERT BOGGESS		305	
	£16.12.1 ½	13264	£26.0.0 1/2
To Mr. WILLIAM PAYNE		20	
To Mr. GARRARD ALEXANDER		124	
To Mr. RICHARD BARNES		90	
To 50 percent on 10.12.1 ½			8.6.0 1/2
1742 Cr.			
By Ballance in Legr. B for 20			0.19.6
By 2 Negro Wenches 1 year 1742		2100	
By Ditto 1743		2000	
By Receiving 40 hogshd. Tobacco @ 10 lb. Tobacco per		400	
By 1 young horse sold JAMES GRINSTED not approved			4.15.0
By Mrs. ANN OSBORN		573	
By 2 Rasons			0.2.6
By 1 pair of silver buckles			0.18.0
1743 By the Crop Tobacco		3130	
1745 By 1 Negro Boy SAM sold JOHN CARLYLE		6180	
By the Inventory of his Estate		14383	6.15.0

At a Court held for Fairfax County September 17th 1745.
RICHARD OSBORN, Gent. Executor of ROBERT OSBORN, deceased exhibited this account against his Estate on oath which is allowed by the Court and admitted to record.   Test   CATESBY COCKE, Clk. Crt.

p.   Fairfax County Will Book 17th September 1745
138   In the name of God Amen. The fourth day of June in the year of our Lord one thousand seven hundred and forty five I REUBIN HALLING of Fairfax County in the Colony of Virginia planter being very sick and weak in body but of perfect mind and memory thanks be given to God therefore calling to mind the mortality of my body and knowing that it is appointed for all men once to die, do make and ordain this my last Will and Testament, That is to say Principally and first of all I give and recommend my soul into the hands of God that gave it and for my body I recommend it to the Earth to be buried in a Christian like and decent manner at the discretion of my Executrix nothing dobting but at the General Resurrection I shall receive the same again by the mighty Power of God And as touching such worldly Estate wherewith it

hath pleased God to bless me in this life I give devise and dispose of the same in the following manner and form Imprimis

I give and bequeath to ELIZABETH my dearly beloved wife moveable Estate to her and her assigns together with my land dureing her life and if it should happen that she should now prove with child then the said Land to be the right and property of the child and its heirs and assigns forever but not to possess the same before the death of my wife ELIZABETH but on the contrary if she be not with child then it is my Will and I do order that the said land after her decease be divided between my Brother ROBERT HALLINGE and JOHN HALLINGE the son of BENJAMIN HALLINGE then their heirs and assigns for ever on the manner following that is to say to my Brother ROBERT thirty acres adjoining to the said ROBERT HALLINGE Land and the remainder to the aforesaid JOHN HALLINGE and by them freely to be possessed and enjoyed and I do hereby utterly disallow revoke and disannul all and every other former Testaments Wills and Legacies Bequest Executors or Executrix except my dearly beloved wife ELIZABETH whome I constitute and appoint as before expressed my sole Executrix of this my last Will and Testament by me in any ways before this time named Willed and bequeathed ratifying and confirming this and no other to be my last Will and Testament. In Witness whereof I have hereunto set my hand and seal the day and year above written.

REUBIN RW [his mark] HALLINGE [seal]

Signed Sealed Published Pronounced and declared by the said REUBIN HALLINGE as his last Will and Testament in the presence of us the Subscribers Vizt.

WADSWORTH WILSON, JOSEPH WILSON, ROBERT ALLEN

p.   Fairfax County Will Book 18th September 1745
139   At a Court held for Fairfax County September 18th 1745.

This last Will and Testament of REUBIN HALLINGE, Deceased was proved in Court by ELIZABETH HALLINGE his widow the Executrix therein who made oath thereto according to Law and the same is proved by WADSWORTH WILSON & JOSEPH WILSON who declared they see ROBERT ALLEN the other Witness thereto subscribed sign the same and admitted to record and on motion of the said ELIZABETH and her performing what is usual in such cases Certificate is granted her for obtaining a probate thereto in due form.   Test   CATESBY COCKE, Clk. Curt.

-Know all men by these presents that we ELIZABETH HALLINGE, DAVID GRIFFETH & DAVID RICHARDSON are held and firmly bound to JOHN COLVILL, Gent. the first Justice in Commission of the Peace for Fairfax County for and in behalf and to the sole use and behoof of the Justices of the said County and their Successors in the sum of two hundred pounds sterling to be paid to the said JOHN COLVILL his Executors and Admrs. jointly and severally firmly by these presents sealed with our seals dated this 18th day of September 1745.

The Condition of this Obligation is such that if the above bound ELIZABETH HALLINGE Executrix of the last Will and Testament of REUBIN HALLINGE deceased do make or cause to be made a true and perfect Inventory of all and singular the Goods Chattels and Credits of the said Deceased which have or shall come to the hands possession or knowledge of the said ELIZABETH or unto the hands or possession or any other person or persons for her and the same so make do exhibit or cause to be exhibited into the County Court of Fairfax at such time as he shall be thereto required by the said Court and the same Goods Chattels and Credits and all other the Goods Chattels and Credits of the said deceased at the time of his death or which at any time after shall come to the hands of possession of the said ELIZABETH or unto the hands or possession of any other person or persons for her do well and truly administer according to Law and further do make a just and true account of her actings and doings therein when thereto required by the said Court and also do well and truly pay and deliver all the Legacies contained and specified in the said Testament as farr as the said Goods Chattels and Credits will thereunto extend and the Law shall charge her for this obligation to be void and of none effect or else to remain in full force and virtue. ELIZABETH ILESABETH HE HALLINGE [seal]

Sealed and Delivered in presence of DAVID X [his mark] GRIFFETH [seal]

DAVID RICHARDSON [seal

ELIZABETH HALLINGE, DAVID GRIFFETH & DAVID RICHARDSON acknowledged this Bond in Fairfax County the 18th day of September 1745 to be their Act and Deed which is admitted to record. Test CATESBY COCKE, Clk. Crt.

p.	Fairfax County Will Book 18th September 1745			
140	The Estate of ROBERT WARDEN Deceased	Dr		
	To 1 Clerks note paid		85	
	To 2 levis		90	
	To CHARLES ANGEL		600	
	To Ditto Ditto		50	0.6.0
	To JOHN HURSK for ketcheing up horses			0.14.0
	To JAMES TIMOTHY			1.0.0
	To FRANCIS ELLZEY for taken up horses			1.1.0
	To HUGH WEST		270	0.14.11 1/2
	To JOHN EVANS		50	
	To RICHARD STURMAN on account of MICHL. MORE		175	
	To JOHN PAGAN		1732	
	To JOHN DALTON		415	0.12.0
	To SARAH McCARTY			0.2.6
	To DANIEL JAMES			0.9.6
	To JOHN CHESSUS		50	0.6.8
	To RICHARD OSBORN		379	
	To Mr. TERREL on account of THOMAS PEARSON			0.17.3 1/2
	To SARAH McCARTY		240	
	To JOHN COLVILL			12.1.10
	To WILLIAM MAYBE 100 lbs. Pork at 2d			0.16.8
	To WILLIAM CLIFTON 1616 paper currency			0.11.0
	To DANIEL FRENCH		50	
	To The Secretarys office		56	
	To 1 Clerks note Gross 150 Nett		120	
			4541	19.15.3
	To my own Account		669	5.2.3
	Per Contra	Cr	5210	24.17.6

Received of JOHN TRAMEL	530	
Ditto of Ditto	877	
Ditto of BRADLEY GARNER	455	
Ditto of FRANCIS ELLZEY		4.12.0
Ditto of CHARLES ANGEL	650	0.6.0
Ditto of JOHN TRAMEL		10.0.0
Ditto of WILLIAM BREWSTER	835	0.8.4
Ditto of DANIEL JAMES		0.11.1
Ditto of WALTER ENGLISH on acct. of JOHN HUTCHISON		0.13.6
Ditto of JOHN JENKINS		0.14.8
Ditto of JOHN TRAMEL		0.10.0
Ditto to 4 hhds Tob. of the Crop	3778	
Ditto of SAMUEL JENKINS		0.18.0
Ditto of a Small Note	183	
Ditto of HENRY SNOW		0.19.0

p.
141

Fairfax County Will Book 18th September 1745

Ditto of ELIZABETH ROSE by JOHN HARLE		0.7.0
Ditto of SAMUEL JENKINS	400	
Ditto Mr. BENONI HALLEY on account of THOMAS ELLEZY		0.5.0
Estate	7708	20.4.7

Errors Excepted this 18th day of September 1745. Per me WILLIAM HARLE
At a Court continued and held for Fairfax County September 18th 1745.
WILLIAM HARLE Executor of ROBERT WARDEN deceased exhibited this account
against his Estate on oath which is allowed by the Court and admitted to record.
Test   CATESBY COCKE, Cl. Crt.

-We WILLIAM HARLE, JOHN LUCAS & JOHN HURST being first sworn before
Capt. JOHN MINOR one of his Majesties Justices for the County of Fairfax hath made
a true and perfect Inventory of the Estate of EDMUND ENGLISH deceased as
followeth Vizt.

To 29 goose at	£2.0.0	To 1 old gun	0.10.0
To 23 ducks at	0.10.0	To 1 spit 1 per old stallards	0.6.0
To 1 mair and colt	3.0.0	To 1 washing tub and turn	
To 1 young horse	1.15.0	pails 1 pigins	0.15.0
To 1 hand saw and a parcel of old		To 2 pots 2 hooks & 1 skillet	0.13.0
coopers tools	0.16.6	To old looking glass sum	
To 1 bead and furniture	5.0.0	old linen	0.3.0
To 1 rug and a parcel of feathers	1.12.0	To chest	0.2.0
To 1 bed stead and cord	0.4.0	To his wareing cloaths	3.0.0
To a parcel of earthenware	0.5.0	To 1 razor 1 hone and sum	
To 1 stone jug and some old		other lumber	0.5.0
Earthenware	0.5.0	To 1 womans side saddle	
To 1 table	0.4.6	and bridle	2.0.0
To 1 trunk	0.3.0	To 5 deer skins	0.10.0
To 1 old table and leather chair	0.3.0	To 1 old bag and sum	
3 old flag ditto		feathers	0.1.6

To 1 box iron and heaters and some old lumber	0.10.0	To 1 bell	0.1.0
To 2 puter pots and a parcel of old boles	0.3.0	To cow & calf and bell	2.0.0
To 5 knives and seven forks	0.2.6	To 1 stear	2.0.0
To 1 bible 2 old books	0.10.6	To 1 cow and yearling	2.15.0
To 1 spice morter and pestle and some old spoons	0.4.0	To 1 cow and heifer	2.10.0
		To 1 saddle	0.7.0
To a parcel of old peuter	0.12.0	To 2 cows & calves	3.0.0
To 1 mair and colt	2.1.6	To 1 addse & sum old tools	0.2.6
To 1 servant man	7.0.0	To 1 old jacket	0.1.0
To 1 young horse	5.0.0	To 1 old pewter dish	1.3.1
			£51.19.9

p. 142   Fairfax County Will Book 15th October 1745
WILLIAM HARLE, JOHN LUCAS, JOHN HURST
At a Court held for Fairfax County October 15th 1745.
This Inventory and appraisement of the Estate of EDMUND ENGLISH deceased was returned and admitted to record.   Test   CATESBY COCKE, Cl. Curt.

-Know all men by these presents that we SAMUEL CANTERBURY, THOMAS FAULKNER & THOMAS CONNEL are held and firmly bound unto JOHN COLVILL, Gent. the first Justice in the Commission of the Peace for Fairfax County for and in behalf and to the sole use and behoof of the Justices of the said County and their Successors in the sum of one hundred pounds sterling to be paid unto the said JOHN COLVILL his Executors Admrs. and assigns to he which payment well and truly to be made we bind ourselves and every of us our and every of our heirs Executors and Admrs. jointly and severally firmly by these presents sealed with our seals dated this xixth day of November 1745.
The Condition of this Obligation is such that is the above bound SAMUEL CANTERBURY Administrator of all the Goods Chattels and Credits of JOHN CULVERHOUSE deceased do make or cause to be made a true and perfect Inventory of all and singular the Goods Chattels or Credits of the said deceased which have or shall come to the hands possession or knowledge of the said SAMUEL CANTERBURY or to the hands or possession of any other person or persons for him and the same so made do exhibit or cause to be exhibited into the County Court of Fairfax at such time as he shall be thereto required by the said Court and the same Goods Chattels and Credits and all other the Goods Chattels and Credits of the said deceased at the time of his death or which at any time after shall come to the hands or possession of the said SAMUEL or unto the hands or possession of any other person or persons for him do make and truly administer according to Law and further do made a Just and true account of his actings and doings therein wen thereto required by the said Court and all the rest and residue of other the said Goods Chattels which shall be found remaining upon the said Admrs. account the same being first examined and allowed by the Justices of the said Court for the time being shall deliver and pay unto such person or persons respectively us the said Justices by their order or Judgment shall direct hereafter appear that any last Will and Testament was made by the said

deceased and the Executor or Executors therein named do exhibit the same into the said Court making request to have it allowed and approved, accordingly if the said SAMUEL being thereunto

p. <u>Fairfax County Will Book 18th February 1745/6</u>

143 required do render and deliver up his Letters of Administration approbation of such Testament being first had and made in the said Court. Then this obligation to be void else to remain in full force and virtue.

ʔ   Sealed and Delivered in presence of

SAMUEL CANTERBURY [seal]

THOMAS FAULKNER [seal]

THOMAS CONNEL [seal]

At a Court held for Fairfax County November the 19th 1745.

SAMUEL CANTERBURY, THOMAS FAULKNER & THOMAS CONNEL acknowledged this Bond to be their act and deed which is admitted to record.

Test CATESBY COCKE, Clk. Crt.

-An Inventory of the Estate of JOHN CULVERHOUSE deceased in Current Money January the 21st 1745.

To a parcel of Carpenters Tools at	£0.9.6
To a parcel of Coopers Tools at	0.8.6
To 1 docking iron at	0.0.6
To 1 gun at	0.10.0
To 1 old saddle and sum other old lumber	0.6.6
To old linen coat two old shirts one pair course linen breeches at	0.9.0
To a parcel of wore out Linen at	0.2.0
To 3 pair of old leather breeches at	0.9.0
To 2 knots of Peach Line and sum other trifels at	0.2.0
To 1 old coat and Jacket at	0.11.0
To 1 Rasor 1 old knife fork 1 old Tobacco Box at	0.2.0
To 1 old Coat and Pladwasteval at	0.3.6
To a parcel of Trifels at	0.0.6
THOMAS FORD	£3.19.6
RICHARD SIMPSON	
ROBERT STEPHENS Praisers	

At a Court held for Fairfax County February 18th 1745.

This Inventory and Appraisement of the Estate of JOHN CULVERHOUSE deceased returned and admitted to record.

Test CATESBY COCKE, Clk. Crt.

-Know all men by these presents that we GARRARD ALEXANDER & WILLIAM HENRY TERRELL are held and firmly bound unto the Worshipful Justices of Fairfax County their Executors and Admrs. in the sum of five hundred pounds sterling to the true payment whereof we bind ourselves our heirs Executors and Admrs. jointly and severally firmly by these presents as Witness our hands and seals this Eighteenth day of February 1745.

p.   Fairfax County Will Book 18th February 1745/6
144   The Condition of the above obligation is such that if the above bound
       GARRARD ALEXANDER Guardian of MARY WADDIE his heirs Executors and
Admrs. do and shall well and truly pay or cause to be well and truly paid unto the said
Orphans all such Estate and Estates as now is or hereafter shall come to the hands
of the said GARRARD as soon as the said Orphan shall attain to Lawfull age or when
thereunto required by the Justices of the Peace of Fairfax County as also save and
keep harmless the said Justices their heirs and Successors from Trouble and
Damage that or may arise about the said Estate then this obligation to be void else in
full force.
               Sealed and Delivered in presence of   GARRARD ALEXANDER [seal]
                                                           WILLIAM HENRY TERRELL [seal]
At a Court held for Fairfax County February 18th 1745.
GARRARD ALEXANDER & WILLIAM HENRY TERRELL, Gent. acknowledged this Bond
to be their Act and Deed which is admitted to record.
               Test   CATESBY COCKE, Cl. Cur.

       -Know all men by these presents that we WILLIAM HENRY TERRELL and
GARRARD ALEXANDER are held and firmly bound unto the worshipfull Justices of
Fairfax County their Executors and Admrs. in the sum of five hundred pounds sterling
to the true payment whereof we bind ourselves our heirs Executors and Admrs. jointly
and severally firmly by these presents as Witness our hands and seals this
Eighteenth day of February 1745.
The Condition of the above obligation is such that if the above bound WILLIAM
HENRY TERRELL Guardian of SIMON PEARSON his heirs Executors and
Admrs. do and shall well and truly pay or cause to be well and truly paid unto the said
Orphans all such Estate and Estates as now is or hereafter shall come to the hands
of the said WILLIAM HENRY as soon as the said Orphan shall attain to Lawfull age or
when thereunto required by the Justices of the Peace of Fairfax County as also save
and keep harmless the said Justices their heirs and Successors from Trouble and
Damage that or may arise about the said Estate then this obligation to be void else in
full force.
               Sealed and Delivered in presence of   WILLIAM HENRY TERRELL [seal]
                                                           GARRARD ALEXANDER [seal]
At a Court held for Fairfax County February 18th 1745.
WILLIAM HENRY TERRELL & GARRARD ALEXANDER, Gent. acknowledged this Bond
to be their Act and Deed which is admitted to record.
               Test   CATESBY COCKE, Cl. Cur.

p.   Fairfax County Will Book 18th February 1745/6
145   -Know all men by these present that we ANN HALLINGE, DAVID RICHARDSON
       & PHILLIP NOLAND are held and firmly bound unto JOHN COLVILL, Gent. the
first Justice of the Commission of the Peace for Fairfax County for and in behalf and
to the sole use and behoof of the Justices of the said County and their Successors in
the sum of fifty pounds sterling to be paid to the said JOHN COLVILL his Executors
and Admrs. and assigns for which payment well and truly to be made we bind

ourselves and every of our heirs Executors and Admrs. jointly and severally firmly by these presents sealed with our seals and dated this 18th day of February 1745. The Condition of this Obligation is such that if the above bound ANN HALLINGE Admrx. of all the Goods Chattels and Credits of BENJAMIN HALLINGE deceased do make or cause to be made a true and perfect Inventory of all and singular the Goods Chattels and Credits of the said Deceased which have or shall come to the hands possession or knowledge of the said ANN or unto the hands or possession of any other person or persons for her and the same do made do exhibit or cause to be exhibited into the County Court of Fairfax at such time as she shall be thereto required by the said Court. And the same Goods Chattels and Credits and all other the Goods and Chattels of the said Deceased at the time of his Death or which at any time after shall come to the hands or possession of the said ANN or unto the hands or possession of any other person or persons for her do well and truly administer according to Law and first her do make a just and true account of her actings and doings therein when thereto required by the said Court and all the rest and residue of the said Goods Chattels and Credits which shall be found and remaining upon the said Admrs. account the same being first examined and allowed by the Justices of the said Court for the time being shall deliver and pay unto such person or persons respectively as the said Justices by their order or judgment shall direct pursuant to the Law in this case made and provided and if it shall hereafter appear that any last Will and Testament was made by the said deceased and the Executor or Executors therein named do exhibit the same into the said Court making request to have it allowed and approved accordingly if the said ANN being thereunto required do render and deliver up her Letters of Administration approbation of such Testament being first had and made in the Court then this obligation to be void else to remain in full force and virtue.

      Sealed and Delivered in presence of   ANN I [her mark] HALLINGE [seal]
                                                      DAVID RICHARDSON [seal]
                                                      PHILIP NOLAND [seal]

At a Court held for Fairfax County February 18th 1745.
ANN HALLINGE, DAVID RICHARDSON & PHILLIP NOLAND acknowledged this Bond to be their Act and Deed which is admitted to record.
                Test   CATESBY COCKE, Cl. Cur.

p.   Fairfax County Will Book 18th February 1745/6
146   -Know all men by these presents that we MARGRET LASSWELL, JACOB
       LASSWELL & ANTHONEY HAMPTON are held and firmly bound unto JOHN
COLVILL, Gent. the first Justice in the Commission of the Peace for Fairfax County for and in behalf and to the sole use and behoof the Justices of the said County and their Successors in the sum of one hundred pounds sterling to be paid to the said JOHN COLVILL his Executors Admrs. and assigns to the which payment well and truly to be made we bind ourselves and every of us our and every of our heirs Executors and Admrs. jointly and severally firmly by these presents sealed with our seals dated this 18th day of February 1745.
The Condition of this obligation is such that if the above named MARGRET LASSWELL, Admrx. of all the Goods Chattels and Credits of JOHN LASSWELL deceased do make or cause to be made a true and perfect Inventory of all and

singular the Goods Chattels and Credits of the said Deceased which have or shall come to the hands possession or knowledge of the said MARGRET or unto the hands or possession of any other person or persons for her and the same so made do exhibit or cause to be exhibited into the County Court of Fairfax at such time as she shall be thereto required by the said Court and the same Goods Chattels and Credits and all other the Goods Chattels and Credits of the said Deceased at the time of his death or which at any time after shall come to the hands or possession of the said MARGRET or unto the hands or possession of any other person or persons for her do well and truly administer accounting so Law and further do make a Just and true account of her actings and doings therein when thereto required by the said Court and all the rest and residue of the said Goods Chattels and Credits which shall be found remaining upon the said Admrs. account the same being first examined and allowed by the Justices of the said Court for the time being shall deliver and pay unto such person or persons respectively as the said Justices by their order or judgment shall direct pursuant to the Law in that case made and provided and if it shall hereafter appear that any last Will and Testament was made by the said Deceased and the Executor or Executors therein named do exhibit the same unto the said Court making request to have it allowed and approved accordingly if the said MARGRET being thereunto required do render and deliver up her Letters of Administration approbation of such Testament being first had and made in the said Court Then this Obligation to be void else to remain in full force and virtue.

Sealed and Delivered in presence of   MARGT. X [her mark] LASSWELL [seal]
JACOB LASSWELL [seal]
ANTHONEY HAMPTON [seal]

p.   Fairfax County Will Book 18th February 1745/6
147   At a Court held for Fairfax County February 18th 1745.
MARGRET LASSWELL, JACOB LASSWELL and ANTHONEY HAMPTON
acknowledged this Bond to be their Act and Deed which is admitted to record.
Test   CATESBY COCKE, Cl. Cur.

-Know all men by these presents that we MARY BROWN, JOHN STURMAN and WILLIAM STURMAN are held and firmly bound unto JOHN COLVILL, Gent. the first Justice in the Commission of the Peace for Fairfax County for and in behalf and to the sole use and behoof the Justices of the said County and their Successors in the sum of two hundred pounds sterling to be paid to the said JOHN COLVILL his Executors Admrs. and assigns to the which payment well and truly to be made we bind ourselves and every of us our and every of our heirs Executors and Admrs. jointly and severally firmly by these presents sealed with our seals dated this 18th day of March 1745.
The Condition of this obligation is such that if the above bound MARY BROWN, Admrx. of all the Goods Chattels and Credits of JAMES BROWN deceased do make or cause to be made a true and perfect Inventory of all and singular the Goods Chattels and Credits of the said Deceased which have or shall come to the hands possession or knowledge of the said MARY or unto the hands or unto the hands or possession of any other person or persons for her do well and truly administer accounting so Law and further do make a Just and true account of her actings and doings therein when

24

thereto required by the said Court and all the rest and residue of the said Goods Chattels and Credits which shall be found remaining upon the said Admrs. account the same being first examined and allowed by the Justices of the said Court for the time being shall deliver and pay unto such person or persons respectively as the said Justices by their order or judgment shall direct pursuant to the Law in that case made and provided and if it shall hereafter appear that any last Will and Testament was made by the said Deceased and the Executor or Executors therein named do exhibit the same unto the said Court making request to have

p.   Fairfax County Will Book 18th March1745/6
148   it allowed and approved accordingly if the said MARY being thereunto required
      do render and deliver up her Letters of Administration approbation of such
Testament being first had and made in the said Court Then this Obligation to be void else to remain in full force and virtue.
       Sealed and Delivered in presence of   MARY X [her mark BROWN [seal]
                                                   JOHN STURMAN [seal
                                                   WILLIAM STURMAN [seal
At a Court held for Fairfax County March 18th 1745.
MARY BROWN, JOHN STURMAN & WILLIAM STURMAN acknowledged this Bond to be their Act and Deed which is admitted to record.
       Test   CATESBY COCKE, Cl. Cur.

       - Know all men by these presents that we JOHN KITCHEN, WILLIAM KITCHEN & WILLIAM SCOTT are held and firmly bound unto JOHN COLVILL, Gent. the first Justice in the Commission of the Peace for Fairfax County for and in behalf and to the sole use and behoof the Justices of the said County and their Successors in the sum of two hundred pounds sterling to be paid to the said JOHN COLVILL his Executors Admrs. and assigns to the which payment well and truly to be made we bind ourselves and every of us our and every of our heirs Executors and Admrs. jointly and severally firmly by these presents sealed with our seals dated this 18th day of March 1745.
The Condition of this obligation is such that if the above bound JOHN KITCHEN Admr. of all the Goods Chattels and Credits of NICHOLAS CARROLL deceased do make or cause to be made a true and perfect Inventory of all and singular the Goods Chattels and Credits of the said Deceased which have or shall come to the hands possession or knowledge of the said JOHN or unto the hands or unto the hands or possession of any other person or persons for him and the same so made do exhibit or cause to be exhibited into the County Court of Fairfax at such time as he shall thereto required by the said Court and the same Goods Chattels and Credits and all other the Goods Chattels and credits of the said deceased at the time of his death or which at anytime after shall come to the hands or possession of the said JOHN or unto the hands or possession of any other person or persons for him do well and truly administer according to Law

p.   Fairfax County Will Book 19th February 1745/6
149   and further do make a Just and true account of his actings and doings therein
      when thereunto required by the said Court and all the rest and residue of the

25

said Goods Chattels and Credits which shall be found remaining upon the said
Admrs. account the same being first examined and allowed by the Justices of the
said Court for the time being shall deliver and pay unto such person or persons
respectively as the said Justices by their order or judgment shall direct pursuant to
the Law in that case made and provided and if it shall hereafter appear that any last
Will and Testament was made by the said Deceased and the Executor or Executors
therein named do exhibit the same unto the said Court making request to have
it allowed and approved accordingly if the said JOHN being thereunto required do
render and deliver up his Letters of Administration approbation of such
Testament being first had and made in the said Court Then this Obligation to be void
else to remain in full force and virtue.

Sealed and Delivered in presence of   JOHN X [his mark] KITCHEN[seal]
                                        WILLIAM W [his mark] KITCHEN [seal]
                                        WILLIAM S [his mark] SCOTT [seal
At a Court held for Fairfax County March xix 1745.
JOHN KITCHEN, WILLIAM KITCHEN & WILLIAM SCOTT acknowledged this Bond to be
their Act and Deed which is admitted to record.
              Test   CATESBY COCKE, Cl. Cur.

-The Estate of SIMON PEARSON	Dr. Sterling Cash	Tobacco
May 21st To 6 yards check 1s 3 yrds bro Linen		
10d whited thread	0.9.5	
To thread 7d per stockings 2s6 q/2 oz.		
Thread ½	0.4.3	
To paid Doct. BRISCOE per attendance and	0.14.5	
Physick to Negro JOE		
To 7 yrds brwon linen per JOE 10d 5s 10d 7 ½		
Yds hessens 9s4 ½ per TOM & LETT	0.15.2 ½	
To 1 felt hat 1 ¾ yds blewfrize 1/7 ½ ½ yd		
Blew Farmey	1.0.4.7 ½	
To 1 yd bron. Linnen 3 yds serge 5s 1 yd bron		
Linnen	0.6.8	
To 2 pr shoes for JOE or TOM 4/6	0.9.0	
To 1 oz. Thread 2 do buttons 7 ½ d 1 stick mohair 2d 0.1.1 ½		
To 2 yds red duffel per negro children 12/ 1 yard 2.0.1.1 ½		
Serge 1/8 ½ yd shattoon		
To Clerks fees paid Majr. COCKE ads ELLZEY		42
1745 To 4 ½ yds Check 3/9 ½ 3 yds brown linnen 2/6 0.6.3 ½		
April		

p. 150	Fairfax County Will Book 15th April 1746		
	at 7s percent	3.1.11 is	885
	To 2/3 of the Publick County and Parish Levys 1744		81
	To 1 boys hat 18 lbs. Tob 19 yds brown linen 142.17		490
	Yds cotten 340		
	To 2 pair boys shoes 58 ½ lbs. Brown thread 15		
	1 boys fine hat 39		112

To ½ yds fine linen 45 3 ¼ yds check 39 ¾

     5 ¼ yards druget 110   184 ¾

To 2 ½ yds shaloon 42 2 yds donlass 30.10 oz thread   75

To 2 doz buttons 15 2 sticks hair 4 ¼ yd buckram 3   22

To paid Mr. BROADWATER for his board   1000

To paid ditto for 4 pair shoes   100

To paid ditto as paid WREN for schooling   100

To 2/3 of Tobacco paid WRIGHT for hhds   93

To 2/3 of hoes paid Mr. BROADWATER   40

To 2/3 of 9 yds Cotten paid ditto   90

To 1 yd ferret & 5 scanes 1 thread   4

To paid DAVID THOMAS for making 2 suits of

     Cloathes & 1 pair breeches for him   0.18.0

March To 3 ½ yds check   30 ½

          At 10 percent   4.16.9 ½   969

                  4318 ¼

To Ballance due to SIMON PEARSON   869 ¾

                  5188

     Contra   Cr.

By your part of GRIMES Rent 1743   0.2.6   353 ½

By your part of Dittos Rent   0.2.6   353 ½

By Mrs. BROADWATER's 1/3 of Negros cloaths   0.10.6   150

By your part of LAY's Rent   353 ½

By Ditto MOSES BALLS   353 ½

By Ditto HENRY COLLOM   353 ½

By ditto WILLIAM DAVIES   487

By ditto RICHARD RICCIA   333

By ditto JOHN HURST   333

By Mrs. BROADWATER 1/3 of Negros cloaths   165 ½

By 2/3 of the Crop 1744   1354

By your part of BROADWATER rent   534

By Mrs. BROADWATER 1/3 Clerks fees ads ELLZEY 10.5.0   50

     Errors Excepted April 15th 1746 per   5188

          WILLIAM HENRY TERRELL

p.   Fairfax County Will Book 15th April 1746

151   At a Court held for Fairfax County April 15th 1746.

     WILLIAM HENRY TERRELL Guardian to SIMON PEARSON exhibited this account against the said Orphans Estate on oath which is allowed and approved by the Court and admitted to record. Test   CATESBY COCKE, Cl. Cur.

     -In Obedience to an order of Fairfax Court we the subscribers being first sworn before LEWIS ELLZEY did meat at the Plantation of JOHN KITCHEN on the 10th day of April 1746 and did appraise all the Estate of NICHOLAS CARROLL deceased as was presented to our view

     To 1 feather bed and bolster old rug and blanket   £1.1.0

     To 1 old bedstead and old cords and two pieces of hides   0.4.0

To 1 old pot and hooks	0.4.0
To 1 old box and padlock old cracked jug	0.3.0
To two old stumps hoes 1 ax 1 old cuting knife	0.2.0
To 1 old frying pan old scimmer old flesh fork and tongs	0.2.0
To 8 lbs. of old puter and 1 old comb	0.3.6
To 2 old jackets 2 pair old breeches	<u>0.16.0</u>
DANIEL SANDERS	£2.15.6
BENONI HALLEY	
LEWIS SANDERS, Junior	

At a Court held for Fairfax County April 15th 1746.
This Inventory and appraisement of the Estate of NICHOLAS CARROLL deceased was returned and admitted to record.   Test   CATESBY COCKE, Cl. Cur.

-Know all men by these presents that we DANIEL FRENCH & DANIEL FRENCH, Junior are held and firmly bound unto the worshipfull Justices of Fairfax County their Executors and Admrs. in the sum of four hundred pounds sterling to the true payment whereof we bind ourselves our heirs Exrs. and Admrs. jointly and severally firmly by these presents Witness our hands and seals this 15th day of April 1746.
The Condition of this Obligation is such that if the above bound DANIEL FRENCH Guardian of MARY WADDIE his heirs Executors and Administrators shall well and truly pay or cause to be well and truly paid unto the said Orphan all such Estate or Estates as now is or hear after shall come to their hands of the said DANIEL as soon as the said Orphan shall attain to Lawfull age or when thereunto required by the Justices of the Peace of Fairfax County

p.   Fairfax County Will Book 15th April 1746
152   as also to save and keep harmless the said Justices their heirs and
        Successors from all trouble and damage that shall or may arrise about the
said Estate then this obligation to be void else in force.
                Sealed and Delivered in the presence of   DANIEL FRENCH [seal]
                                                            DANIEL FRENCH [seal]
At a Court held for Fairfax County April 15th 1746.
DANIEL FRENCH & DANIEL FRENCH, Junior, Gent. acknowledged this Bond to be their act and deed which is admitted to record. Test   CATESBY COCKE, Cl. Curt.

-The Estate of JEREMIAH BRONAUGH, deceased   Dr
1744 Aug 11

To paid WILLIAM CHAMPNEYS	0.9.0
To paid HENRY BOGGESS	0.5.0
To paid ROBERT BOGGESS	2.0.1
To paid BENJAMIN ADAMS	2.13.10 1/4
To paid OWEN GILMORE	0.18.7
To paid HUGH MITCHEL	29.8.7
To paid WILLIAM REARDON	1.6.3
To paid JOHN BAXTER	1.11.5
To paid JAMES JARVIS	0.5.3
To paid THOMAS BOSMAN	0.5.0

To paid MOSES BOTTS				0.1.6
To paid EBENEZER MORS				3.4.11
To paid MARY BOSMAN	Tobacco		533	
To paid Maj. COCKE			424	
To paid WILLIAM PAYNE			80	
To paid EDWARD BARRY				0.7.6
To paid JOSIAH FARGUSON				0.15.0
To paid Mr. Secretary CARTER			36	
To paid Mr. Secretary NELSON			36	
To paid ROBERT LINZA			800	
To paid Mrs. ANN MASON			1260	
To paid JAMES GUTHRIE				3.19.9
To paid 3 Levys			144	
To my Expences and trouble as Administrator				4.18.0

p.
153

<u>Fairfax County Will Book 20th May 1746</u>

To paid the Reverend Mr. GREEN			<u>6</u>	
Per Contra	Cr		3319	
By the sale of the Estate				96.13.1
By the Crops of Tobacco			4898	
By Cash				9.17.5
By Cash				0.12.7

Errors Excepted by DAVID BRONAUGH

At a Court held for Fairfax County May 20th 1746.

DAVID BRONAUGH Administrator of JEREMIAH BRONAUGH deceased acknowledged this account against his Estate on oath which is allowed by the Court and admitted to record.　　Test　　　CATESBY COCKE, Cl. Cur.

-1745 The Estate of MR. JOHN HEREFORD deceased		Dr tob	
To Cash paid WILLIAM EILEBECK	No1		14.9.11 1/2
To paid Mr. NEAL Paper Money	No3		0.14.4
To paid ditto	No4	2180	
To paid JOHN ASHFORD	No5		1.10.0
To paid THOMAS BOSMAN	No6		2.3.11 1/2
To paid RICHARD STURMAN	No7		0.14.7
To paid MOSES LINTON	No8		0.8.0
To paid SAMUEL WILSON	No9		0.6.0
To paid JAMES JARVIS	No10		0.18.0
To paid Doctor HART	No 11		1.1.6
To paid HENRY THRELKELD	No12		1.3.10 1/2
To paid ROBERT BOGGESS	No13		1.1.7 1/2
To paid Mr. MOSS	14		1.8.0 1/2
To paid EDWARD WASHINGTON	15		0.1.3
To paid WILLIAM CLAIR	16		2.6.0
To paid ROBERT BOGGESS for Levys	17	435	
To paid JOHN BRONAUGH	18	100	
To paid JOSEPH CASH	19	250	

To a Clerks note	20	200
To a Secretarys note	21	36
To paid Mr. BARRY	22	328
To paid JOSEPH REID	23	75

p. 154	<u>Fairfax County Will Book 20th May 1746</u> To paid Mr. McCARTY	3.9.7
	Per Contra Cr	
	By Cash Received	20.5.11 3/4
	By the Amount of the Inventory	149.12.2

At a Court held for Fairfax County May 20th 1746.
JANE HEREFORD Executrix of JOHN HEREFORD deceased exhibited this account against his Estate on oath which is allowed by the Court and admitted to record.
Test   CATESBY COCKE, Cl. Cur.

-Fairfax   We the Subscribers whose names are under written being first sworn have praised and valured all and singular the Estate of BENJAMIN HALLINGE deceased as came to our view &c

One Coat and one pair of breeches	1.5.0
To 1 coat and jacket	1.0.6
To 1 pair of shars and knifes and other things	0.5.0
To common pray book	0.2.0
To 1 bottle and some talour	0.3.6
2 persons 1 tinpan 4 spoons	0.4.6
2 crackt eathing pans & other trwels	0.4.0
1 pair of old books and 4 pair of hames & collon	0.2.0
Some nails & an old sadle	0.12.0
To a pasel of old dear skins	0.11.0
To 1 crackt pot and old pale	0.2.6
To 1 Rogg and blanket and bed tick and boldster	1.0.0
3 stools and old table	0.1.0
2 pistols 1 old gun and one barrel of gun	2.5.0
2 weeding hoes and 1 ax and hatchet	0.4.6
2 sides of leather	0.3.6
1 bedstid	0.5.0
1 old black horse 4 of 1 yowling 2 of	3.0.0
1 black mair and colt	4.0.0
1 bay mair and colt	2.0.0

p. 155	<u>Fairfax County Will Book 20th May 1746</u>
1 old black ditto and colt	1.15.0
1 cow and yowling	1.10.0
1 cow and calf and yowling	1.15.0
1 stair 20s and a heifer 10s	<u>1.10.0</u>
	£29.1.0
To 1 Bull 3 years old	1.6.0
3 Sows 9 shoats and eleven pigs	<u>3.0.0</u>

Carried over	£28.7.0
1 hide 1 dear skin and old bagg	0.6.0
1 lad has seven months to serve	2.10.0
THOMAS AWBREY	£31.3.0
JOHN WILKE	
JOHN GORDON	

At a Court held for Fairfax County May 20th 1746.
This Inventory and appraisement of the Estate of BENJAMIN HALLINGE deceased was returned and admitted to record.   Test   CATESBY COCKE, Cl. Cur.

-According to an order of Court to us directed we have praised all and singular the Goods and Chattels of the Estate of JOHN RICHARDSON brought before us whose names are under written.

To 9 hogs	2.10.0
To 1 horse one yearling 15s	3.0.0
To Cow and Calf	2.0.5
To 2 axes	0.5.0
To 2 Augers 4s 3 hand saws 5s	0.9.0
To 1 gauge 1/ and 4 chisels 2/6	0.3.6
To 1 drawing knife 2/ a parsil of old iron	0.3.6
To 2 wedges one logerhead smoothing iron	0.5.0
To a parcel 4d nails 6d 1 jonter 1/6	0.2.0
To 4 Gimblits 1 pair fleams and pair sisers	0.2.0
To 2 files 1 set 1 rule 4/6 2 hamers 3 knives 1 plain iron 2s	
2 sturraps irons horseshoe 6d	0.7.0
To 1 basket and old nails 1/ 1 coopers adze 1 compasses	
1 coopers ax 1 howel and cutting knife	0.7.0
To the Rest of the Coopers tools	0.3.0
To 2 mill picks and one old pail	0.2.0

p.
156 Fairfax County Will Book 20th May 1746

To 1 hooke and coulter 5s swingle tree iron 1 coller and hames	0.7.0
To 2 irons 4s 1 bell and bell coller 3s	0.7.0
To 1 old sadle and old bridle 7s 1 old spade 1/6	0.9.6
To the shoemakers tools 5s 5 glass bottles and vials 2 pair	
Kniting neddles	0.7.0
To a parsel of old puter 5s 1 dish 4d	6.5.4
To 2 coolers piggin 1 old sifter	0.4.0
To 1 frian pan 2s s pooks & 2 poot hooks 10s	0.12.0
To a parcel of old books 3/6 1 rasor and pen knife 1 cup	0.4.6
To 1 pair spectacles 6d 1 grinding stone 8s & 1 bell	0.8.6
To 2 stools & 1 old table 4d to bedsted and beding	0.17.10
To Tan'd leather 2s 1 old weeding hoe	0.2.6
To 3 old tubs 3 one horse hide 2/6 to some leather and pestle	0.6.0
To 1 howel and mattock	0.2.6
JOSIAS CLAPHAM	£14.12.3
HUGH H [his mark] FOUCH	

PHILLIP NOLAND

At a Court held for Fairfax County May 20th 1746.
This Inventory and appraisement of the Estate of JOHN RICHARDSON deceased was returned and admitted to record.   Test   CATESBY COCKE, Cl. Cur.

-Fairfax County   In Obedience to an order of Court we whose names are under written being first sworn have appraised and valued all and singular the Estate of REUBIN HALLINGE deceased that came to hour view &c.

To 1 sow and 6 pigs 12s To 1 small cow and calf 35s	
To 1 pot 8 gallons	2.19.0
To 1 old pale and old piggin and weeding how 5s to 1 sadle 15s	
To 2 new basons 8s	1.8.0
To 1 Razor and knife and fork and knee buckles 2/6 to 1 pair	
Of shoes 4/6	0.7.0
To 1 new coat vest & breeches £3 to and old coat 3/6 to 1 hat 3/3	3.6.6
To 1 cheek shirt 7s to 2 old blankets 8s	0.13.0
To 1 mare and colt 14.10 to 1 sow 8/ & six shoats 30s	6.8.0
THOMAS AWBREY	15.3.6
PHILIP NOLAND	
JOHN WILKIE	

At a Court held for Fairfax County May 20th 1746.
This Inventory and appraisement of the Estate of REUBIN HALLINGE deceased was returned and admitted to record.   Test   CATESBY COCKE, Cl. Cur.

p.   Fairfax County Will Book 20th May 1746

157   -In obedience to an order of Fairfax County Court we the subscribers have returned the Inventory of the Estate of JOHN LASSWELL deceased offered to us as followeth Vizt.

To 2 old hand saws and a rest	0.2.6
To one old cross cut saw	0.2.6
To one broad ax	0.3.0
To 1 old whip saw tiller and file	0.14.0
To 1 spade 1 adze 2 old axes 1 grubing hoe and drawing knife	0.6.9
To 1 Linnen wheel at 7s	0.7.0
To 1 iron and old beem knife	0.2.6
To 1 old woolf trup	0.6.0
To 4 old planes 1 iron square 1 rule 1 spoke shave	0.5.0
To 3 augers 1 gouge 4 turners hooks 1 broad chissel 1 mare	
2 maudrels	0.8.0
To 1 Coopers adze 2 crooses 1 pair compasses	0.2.6
To 1 old jute saddle 2 chears 2 realst hachet	0.3.0
To 1 old broad hoe 1 frying pan 2 sickles	0.3.10
To 1 small box of cobblers tools	0.0.2
To 1 old bull	0.5.0
To 1 cow lame in the bogg	1.0.0
To 2 steers of 2 years old	3.0.0
To 2 sick cows and caves	1.0.0

To 1 heffer and calf 25s to 1 2 year old ditto 15s	2.0.0
To 1 cow big with calf and one eartin	2.0.0
To 2 Ewes and 2 lambs	1.0.0
To 1 mair and earlin colt	2.0.0
To 1 horse £4 to 2 sows 3 shoats and five piggs 24s	5.4.0
To 1 mair and colt	3.0.0
To 3 bells 8s to 1 old one ditto and two wedges 4s	0.12.0
To a parcel of old iron	0.2.6
To 73 lbs. of pot iron at 2d per pound	0.12.2
To a parcel of old puter 7# at 6d pr pound	0.3.5
To a parcel of old books 1 ink pot 1 earthen bottle	0.5.0
To 1 churn and some of piggins	0.2.6
To 1 bed 1 blanket and 3 old ruggs	0.15.0
To 1 rifle gun £3 1 small gun and 1 barrel 10s	3.10.0

p.
158

Fairfax County Will Book 20th May 1746

To a parcel of old smiths tools	0.1.0
To 2 small hides and three pieces	0.8.0
To 1 pair of hand mill stones	0.15.0
WALTER WILLIAMS	33.0.8
JOHN MIDDLETON	

An account of Goods sold before praisd
To one horse at 900# tobacco   HENRY HAMPTON

To 2 cows	4.0.0
To 900$ Tobacco made cash at 1s6 percent	5.2.6
	9.2.6

At a Court held for Fairfax County May 20th 1746.   33.0.8
This Inventory and appraisement of the Estate of JOHN LASSWELL   42.3.2
Deceased was returned and admitted to record.   Test   CATESBY COCKE, Cl. Cur.

-Know all men by these presents that we WILLIAM BRONAUGH, HENRY RARDON, DAVID JONES and GILES TILLETT are held and firmly bound unto JOHN COLVILL, Gent. the first Justice of the Commission of the peace for Fairfax County for and in behalf and to the sole use and behoof of the Justices of the said County and their Successors in the sum of three hundred pounds sterling to be paid to the said JOHN COLVILL his Executors and Administrators and assigns to the which payment well and truly to be made we bind ourselves and every of us our and every of our heirs Exrs. and administrators jointly and severally firmly by these presents sealed with our seals dated this xx day of May 1746.
The Condition of this obligation is such that if the above bound WILLIAM BRONAUGH Administrator of all the Goods Chattels and Credits of DAVID BATHENS deceased do make or cause to be made a true and perfect Inventory of all and singular the Goods Chattels and Credits of the said Deceased which have or shall come to the hands possession or knowledge of the said WILLIAM or unto the hands or possession of any other person or persons for him and the same so made do exhibit or cause to be exhibited into the County Court of Fairfax at such time as he shall be thereto required by the said Court and the same Goods Chattels and credits and all other the Goods

Chattels and Credits of the said Deceased at the time of his death or which at any time after shall come to the hands or possession of the said WILLIAM or unto

p.   Fairfax County Will Book 20th May 1746
159   the hands or possession of any other person or persons for him do well and truly administer according to Law and further do make a just and true account of his actings and doings therein when thereto required by the said Court and all the rest and residue of the said Goods Chattels and Credits which shall be found remaining upon the said Administrators account the same being first examined and allowed by the Justices of the said Court for the time being shall deliver and pay unto such person or persons respectively as the said Justices by their order or judgment shall direct pursuant to the Law in that case made and provided and if it shall hereafter appear that any last Will and Testament was made by the said Deceased and the Executor or Executors therein named do exhibit the same into the said Court making request to have it allowed and approved accordingly if the said WILLIAM being thereunto required do render and deliver up his Letters of Administration approbation of such Testament being first had and made in the said Court then this obligation to be void else to remain in full force and virtue.

Sealed and Delivered in presence of   WILLIAM x [his mark] BRONAUGH [seal]
                                          HENRY HR [his mark] RARDON [seal]
                                          DAVID JONES [seal]
                                          GILES TILLETT [seal]
At a Court held for Fairfax County May 20th 1746.
WILLIAM BRONAUGH, HENRY RARDON, DAVID JONES and GILES TILLETT acknowledged this Bond to be their Act and Deed which is admitted to record.
        Test   CATESBY COCKE, Clk. Cur.

-Know all men by these presents that we MARY CUMTON, JOHN WEST and NICHOLAS MARTIN are held and firmly bound unto JOHN COLVILL, Gent. the first Justice in the Commission of the peace for Fairfax County for and in behalf and to the sole use and behoof of the Justices of the said County and their Successors in the sum of one hundred pounds sterling to be paid to the said JOHN COLVILL his Executors Administrators and assigns to the which payment well and truly to be made we bind ourselves and every of us our and every of our heirs Executors and administrators jointly and severally firmly by these presents sealed with our seals dated this xx day of May 1746.
The Condition of this obligation is such that if the above bound MARY CUMTON Administratrix of all the Goods Chattels and Credits of JOHN CUMTON deceased do make or cause to be made a true and perfect Inventory of all and singular the Goods Chattels and Credits of the said Deceased which

p.   Fairfax County Will Book 20th May 1746
160   have or shall come to the hands possession of knowledge of the said MARY or unto the hands or possession of any other person or persons for her and the same so made do exhibit or cause to be exhibited into the County Court of Fairfax at such time as he shall be thereto required by the said Court and the same Goods Chattels and Credits and all other the Goods Chattels and Credits of the said

Deceased at the time of his death or which at any time after shall come to the hands or possession of the said MARY or unto the hands or possession of any other person or persons for her do well and truly administer according to Law, and further do make a just and true account of her actings and doings therein when thereto required by the said Court and all the Rest and Residue of the said Goods Chattels and Credits which shall be found remaining upon the said Administratrix's account the same being first examined and allowed by the Justices of the said Court for the time being shall deliver and pay unto such person or persons respectively as the said Justices by their order or Judgment shall direct pursuant to the same in that case made and provided and if it shall hereafter appear that at any last Will and Testament was made by the said Deceased and the Executor or Executors therein named do exhibit the same into the said Court making request to have it allowed and approved, accordingly if the said MARY being thereunto required do render and deliver up her Letters of Administration approbation of such Testament being first had and made in the said court then this obligation to be void else to remain in full force and virtue.

Sealed and Delivered in the presence of   MARY CM [her mark] CUMTON [seal]
JOHN WEST [seal]
NICHOLAS N [his mark] MARTIN [seal]

At a Court held for Fairfax County May 20th 1746.
MARY CUMTON, JOHN WEST and NICHOLAS MARTIN acknowledged this Bond to be their Act and Deed which is admitted to record.   Test   CATESBY COCKE, Cl. Cur.

p.   Fairfax County Will Book 20th May 1746

161	-The Estate of WILLIAM WILLIAMS deceased	Dr	
	To funeral expences		2.0.0
	To Clerks fees	120# tobacco	
	To Secretarys ditto	36	
	To paid JAMES JARVIS by account proved		1.4.2
	To ditto HUGH MITCHEL by ditto		5.14.9
	To ditto MOSES LINTON		0.3.2
	To Ditto SILAS LITTLE JOHN		1.1.9
	To paid Mr. JAMES BAXTER for rent	524	
	To paid Mr. WILLIAM PAYNE for county and publick Levys	72	
	To paid Mr. BOGGESS for Parish levys	50	
	To paid Maj. GRAYSON by account proved		1.1.5
	To an Attorneys fee		0.15.0
	To appraisers fees	80	
	To paid Mr. GODFREY for helping with the Crop of Tobacco		0.3.9
	To the Warehouse 3 days a Work		
	To paid ditto for 3 hogsheads	90	
	To my own and Childrens trouble in striping and carrying		1.0.0
	The Tobacco to the Warehouse		
	To paid the Inspectors for prizeing		0.2.6
	To paid JOSEPH REID by account proved	75	0.0.11 1/2
	To paid Mr. ROBERT BOGGESS by ditto		2.6.0 3/4
	Pr Contra Cr		
	By the amount of the Inventory		£13.1.1

By his Crop of Tobacco   1331
           Errors Excepted by ELIZABETH WILLIAMS, Admrx.
At a Court held for Fairfax County May 20th 1746.
ELIZABETH WILLIAMS, Admrs. of WILLIAM WILLIAMS deceased exhibited this account
against his Estate on oath which is allowed by the Court and admitted to record.
           Test   CATESBY COCKE, Cl. Cur.

p.   Fairfax County Will Book 21st May 1746
162   -I JOHN HALLING of Truro Parish in the County of Fairfax Yeoman being at this
       time in good and perfect memory tho the mercy of God, do make this my last
Will and Testament in manner following that is to say.
Item I leave to my Cosen ARON RICHARDSON eighty acres of land I now live upon to
him and his heirs forever, but if he should dy without issue my Will is that it be equll
devided between my too cosins AMOSS RICHARDSON and DAVID RICHARDSON,
Junior and their heirs forever but if one of them should dy before they come of age
the other to injoy his part of the land and DAVID RICHARDSON and his wife MARY to
have their lives in the said lands if they will come and live on it adureing their lives.
Item I leave my brother ROBERT HALLING all that part of Land fell to me by the death
of my Brother ARON HALLING the same I leave to him and his heirs and assigns
forever.
Item I leave my two brothers ROBERT HALLING and JOHN SINKLER one young mair
and cow yowling a peace to have then Immeadly after my death.
Item I leave all the remainder of my lands and moveable Estate to be equall devided
between my Brothers BENJAMIN HALLING and ROBART HALLING and my sisters
MARY RICHARDSON and ELIZABETH HARRIS and JOHN SINKLER and HANNAH
SINKLER all the above Estate I leave to them and their heirs and assigns forever.
Item Lastly I do make and constitute DAVID RICHARDSON my hole and sole Executrix
of this my last Will and Testament. In Witness my hand and seal this 9th day of March
1744/5.   JOHN HALLING [sea]
      Signed Sealed and Delivered in the presence of us
      THOMAS AWBREY, JOHN WILKE, OWEN [his mark] McGARR
At a Court held for Fairfax County May 21st 1746.
The within last Will and Testament of JOHN HALLING Deceased

p.   Fairfax County Will Book 22nd May 1746
163   was proved by the oaths of THOMAS AWBREY and JOHN WILKIE who declared
       they did see OWEN McGARR sign the same as a Witness and ordered to be
       Certified.   Test   CATESBY COCKE, Cl. Cur.
At a Court continued and held for Fairfax County May 22nd 1746.
This Will was made oath to according to Law by DAVID RICHARDSON the Executor
Therein named, And on his motion and performing what is usual in such cases
Certificate is granted him for obtaining a probate thereof in due form.
      Test   CATESBY COCKE, Cl. Cur.

     -Know all men by these presents that we DAVID RICHARDSON, WILLIAM
HARLE and GARRARD TRAMMEL are held and firmly bound unto JOHN COLVILL, Gent.
the first Justice in the Commission of the peace for Fairfax County for and in behalf

and to the sole use and behoof of the Justices of the said County and their Successors in the sum of three hundred pounds sterling to be paid to the said JOHN COLVILL his Executors Administrators and assigns to the which payment well and truly to be made we bind ourselves and every of us our and every of our heirs Exrs. and Admrs. jointly and severally firmly by these presents sealed with our seals dated the 22nd day of May 1746.

The Condition of this obligation is such that if the above bound DAVID RICHARDSON Executor of the last Will and Testament of JOHN HALLING deceased do make or cause to be made a true and perfect Inventory of all and singular the Goods Chattels and Credits of the said Deceased which have or shall come to the hands possession or knowledge of the said DAVID or unto the hands or possession of any other person or persons for him and the same so made do exhibit or cause to be exhibited into the County Court of Fairfax at such time as he shall be thereto required by the said Court and the same Goods Chattels and Credits and all other the Goods Chattels and Credits of the said Deceased at the time of his Death or which at any time after shall come to the hands or possession of the said DAVID or unto the hands or possession of any other person or persons for him do well and truly administer according to Law and further do make a just and true account of their actings and doings therein wen thereunto required by the said Court and do well and truly pay and deliver all the Legacies contained and specified in the said Testament as farr as the said Goods Chattels and Credits will thereunto extend and

p. Fairfax County Will Book 22nd May 1746
163 the Law shall charge him then this Obligation to be void and of none effect or else to remain in full force and vertue
Sealed and Delivered in the presence of   DAVID RICHARDSON [seal]
WILLIAM H [his mark] HARLE [seal]
GARRARD IT [his mark] TRAMMEL [seal]

At a Court continued and held for Fairfax County May 22nd 1746.
DAVID RICHARDSON, WILLIAM HARLE & GARRARD TRAMMEL acknowledged this Bond to be their Act and Deed which is admitted to record.
Test   CATESBY COCKE, Cl. Curt.

-Know all men by these presents that I JOHN LITTLETON of the parish of Truro and County of Fairfax planter being very sick and weak of body but of sound mind, blessed be God therefore do make the following disposall of my effects Vizt. Imprimis I give and bequeath unto my beloved wife SARAH the plantation where she now liveth with half the tract of Land being one hundred and twenty five acres and after her decrease to my son SOLOMON and his heirs forever.
Item I give and bequeath unto my son CHARLES the remaining part of my Land to him and his heirs forever and in case he should dye without heirs I mean heirs of his body Lawfully begotten, it is my will that his part of my land should descend unto my Cousin WILLIAM LITTLETON and to his heirs forever, and it is my desire that the devision of my Land be made thus Vizt. to being at the spring branch and a course set from thence to hit the Line and make an equal Devision.
Item I will and bequeath unto my Cousin WILLIAM one musket.

37

This I do publish and declare to be my last Will and Testament, revoking all other and former Wills and Testaments, dated October 1ˢᵗ 1745.

Signed and Delivered and published to be my last Will and Testament in presence of   HENRY H [his mark] TREN   JOHN X [his mark] LITTLETON [seal]
WILLIAM X [his mark] LITTLETON
ZEPHA. WADE

p.   Fairfax County Will Book 17ᵗʰ June 1746
165   At a Court held for Fairfax County Aprill 15ᵗʰ 1746.

This last Will and Testament of JOHN LITTLETON deceased was proved by the oaths of HENRY TREN and WILLIAM LITTLETON and ordered to be Certified.
Test   CATESBY COCKE, Cl. Cur.
At a Court held for Fairfax County June 17ᵗʰ 1746.
The within last Will and Testament of JOHN LITTLETON was made oath to by SARAH LITTLETON according to Law [ZEPHANIAH WADE the other Witness thereto being dead] and on motion of the said SARAH and her performing what is usual in such cases Certificate is granted him for obtaining Letters of Administration with the said Will annexed in due form.   Test   CATESBY COCKE, Cl. Cur.

-Know all men by these presents that we SARAH LITTLETON, WILLIAM PAYNE and JOSEPH GARDNER are held and firmly bound unto unto JOHN COLVILL, Gent. the first Justice in the Commission of the peace for Fairfax County for and in behalf and to the sole use and behoof of the Justices of the said County and their Successors in the sum of one hundred pounds sterling to be paid to the said JOHN COLVILL his Executors Administrators and assigns to the which payment well and truly to be made we bind ourselves and every of us our and every of our heirs Executors and Admrs. jointly and severally firmly by these presents sealed with our seals dated this 17ᵗʰ June 1746.
The Condition of this Obligation is such that if the above bound SARAH LITTLETON Admrx. with the last Will and Testament of JOHN LITTLETON deceased thereunto annexed, do make it cause to be made a true and perfect Inventory of all and singular the Good Chattels and Credits of the said deceased which have or shall come to the hands possession or knowledge of the said SARAH or unto the hands or possession of any other person or persons for her and the same so made do exhibit or cause to be exhibited into the County Court of Fairfax at such times as she shall be thereto required by the said Court and the same Goods Chattels and Credits and all other the Goods Chattels and Credits of the said Deceased at the time of his death or which at any time after shall come to the hands or possession of the said SARAH or unto the hands or possession of any other person or persons for her do well and truly administer according to law and further do make a just and true account of her actings and doings therein when thereunto required by the said Court and also do well and truly pay and deliver all the Legacies contained and specified in the said Testament as farr as the said Goods Chattels and Credits will thereunto extend and the Law shall charge her then the Obligation to be void else to remain in full force and vertue.
Sealed and Delivered in presence of   SARAH X [her mark] LITTLETON [seal]
WILLIAM PAYNE [seal]

p.   Fairfax County Will Book 17th June 1746

166   At a Court held for Fairfax County June 17th 1746.

SARAH LITTLETON, WILLIAM PAYNE & JOSEPH GARDNER acknowledged this Bond to be their Act and Deed which is admitted to record.

Test   CATESBY COCKE, Cl. Cur.

-Know all men by these presents that we DANIEL MILLS, WILLIAM GRIMES and WILLIAM DAVIE are held and firmly bound unto JOHN COLVILL, Gent. the first Justice in the Commission of the peace for Fairfax County for and in behalf and to the sole use and behoof of the Justices of the said County and their Successors in the sum of one hundred pounds sterling to be paid to the said JOHN COLVILL his Executors Administrators and assigns to the which payment well and truly to be made we bind ourselves and every of us our and every of our heirs Executors and Admrs. jointly and severally firmly by these presents sealed with our seals dated this 17th June 1746. The Condition of this Obligation is such that if the above bound DANIEL MILLS Admr. of all the Goods Chattels and Credits of JUDITH BALLINGER deceased do make or cause to be made a true and perfect Inventory of all and singular the Good Chattels and Credits of the said deceased which have or shall come to the hands possession or knowledge of the said DANIEL or unto the hands or possession of any other person or persons for him and the same so made do exhibit or cause to be exhibited into the County Court of Fairfax at such time as he shall be thereto required by the said Court and the same Goods Chattels and Credits and all other the Goods Chattels and Credits of the said Deceased at the time of his death or which at any time after shall come to the hands or possession of the said DANIEL or unto the hands or possession of any other person or persons for him do well and truly administer according to law and further do make a just and true account of his actings and doings therein when thereunto required by the said Court and all the rest and residue of the said Goods Chattels and Credits which shall be found remaining upon the said Admrs. account the same being first

p.   Fairfax County Will Book 17th June 1746

167   examined and allowed by the Justices of the said Court for the time being shall deliver and pay unto such person or persons respectively as the said Justices by their order or judgment shall direct pursuant to the Law in that case made and provided and if it shall hereafter appear that any last Will and Testament was made by the said Deceased and the Executor or Executors therein named do exhibit the same into the said Court making request to have it allowed and approved accordingly if the said DANIEL being thereunto required do render and deliver up his Letters of Administration approbation of such Testament being first had and made in the said Court Then this Obligation to be void else to remain in full force and vertue.

Sealed and Delivered in presence of   DANIEL D [his mark] MILLS [seal]

WILLIAM [his mark] GRIMES [seal]

WILLIAM [his mark] DAVIE [seal]

At a Court held for Fairfax County June 17th 1746.

DANIEL MILLS, WILLIAM GRIMES and WILLIAM DAVIE acknowledged this Bond to be their Act and Deed which is admitted to record.   Test   CATESBY COCKE, Cl. Cur.

-In the name of God Amen I HENRY OKEAN of the Parish of Truro in the County of Fairfax Planter being of a present and disposing mind and memory do ordain make publish and declare this my last Will and Testament thereby revoking all former Wills and Testaments by me made in manner and form following, Imprimis I commend my soul unto the hands of the Allmighty God my body to the earth to be buried in a decent manner at the Discretion of my Executors,

Item I give and bequeath unto my dear loveing wife JENNY two feather beds and furniture seven dishes fifteen plates five pewter basons two tin pans two iron potts three gunns two tables two chests one mans old saddle one pen snaffle bridle 1 pewter tankard six horse three mares one two years old colt one yearling colt one bleane faced horse and young mare strayed away from the Plantation where I now live and branded with HC seven cows four calves and eight yearlings ten sows and pigs eight young hogs Tobacco in Mr. CARLYLES hands five thousand six hundred seventy six pounds and left in his hands last year at setteling seven pounds cash one Negro fellow named JACK and another named GAWAH during her natural life and after her decease to RICHARD OKEAN or his heirs lawfully

p.   Fairfax County Will Book 15th July 1746
168   begotten now living in Lancaster County Pensilvania without nearer heirs comes into the Country,

Item I have one Negro whench named RACHEL which I set free from me and my heirs forever.

Item I give and bequeath unto JOHN LOE an Orphan boy now under our care one cow and calf one young horse bridle and saddle amen suite of cloaths and everything suitable the right of the Land we now live upon after my wifes death.

Item I give and bequeath unto SARAH HURST the daughter of JOHN HURST, Junior one young cow and a young son,

Item I give and bequeath unto JOHN DISKINS son of DANIEL DISKINS a young cow and calf,

Item I give and bequeath unto WILLIAM BOLING my suit of Dueroy cloaths and a gun he now has Thereby nominate made ordain and appoint my wife JENNY and Capt. JOHN MINOR, Gent. Executors of this my last Will and Testament injoining them to see my body decently buried my Debts and Legacies truly paid and satisfied and my will in all things faithfully performed. In witness I have published and declared this my last Will and Testament and thereto have set my hand seal the 2nd day of June in the year of our Lord 1746.   HENRY H [his mark] OKEAN [seal]
    Signed Sealed Published and declared in the presence of
    DAVID THOMAS, MOSES BALL, CHARLES MASON
At a Court held for Fairfax County July 15th 1746.
This last Will and Testament of HENRY OKEAN deceased was presented in Court by JENNY OKEAN the Executrix therein named who made oath thereto according to Law and the same is proved by DAVID THOMAS, MOSES BALL and CHARLES MASON witnesses thereto and admitted to record and on motion of the said Executrix and her performing what is usual in such cases Certificate is granted her for obtaining a Probate thereof in due form.
    Test   CATESBY COCKE, Cl. Cur.

p.   Fairfax County Will Book 15th July 1746

169   -Know all men by these presents that we JENNY OKEAN, MICHAEL REGAN & WILLIAM BOLING are held and firmly bound unto JOHN COLVILL, Gent. the first Justice in the Commission of the peace for Fairfax County for and in behalf and to the sole use and behoof of the Justices of the said County and their Successors in the sum of three hundred pounds sterling to be paid to the said JOHN COLVILL his Executors Administrators and assigns to the which payment well and truly to be made we bind ourselves and every of us our and every of our heirs Executors and Admrs. jointly and severally firmly by these presents sealed with our seals dated this 15th July 1746.

The Condition of this Obligation is such that if the above bound JENNY OKEAN, Exrx. of the last Will and Testament of HENRY OKEAN deceased do make or cause to be made a true and perfect Inventory of all and singular the Good Chattels and Credits of the said deceased which have or shall come to the hands possession or knowledge of the said JENNY or unto the hands or possession of any other person or persons for her and the same so made do exhibit or cause to be exhibited into the County Court of Fairfax at such time as she shall be thereto required by the said Court and the same Goods Chattels and Credits and all other the Goods Chattels and Credits of the said Deceased at the time of his death or which at any time after shall come to the hands or possession of the said JENNY or unto the hands or possession of any other person or persons for her do well and truly administer according to law and further do make a just and true account of her actings and doings therein when thereunto required by the said Court and also do well and truly pay and deliver all the Legacies contained and specified in the said Testament as farr as the said Goods Chattels and Credits will therein extend and the Law shall charge her. Then this obligation to be void and of none effect or else to remain in full force and vertue.

Sealed and Delivered in presence of   JENNY H [her mark] OKEAN [seal]
                                             MICHAEL REAGAN [seal]
                                             WILLIAM BOLING [seal]

At a Court held for Fairfax County July 15th 1746.
JENNY OKEAN, MICHAEL REAGAN and WILLIAM BOLING acknowledged this Bond to be their Act and Deed which is admitted to record.   Test CATESBY COCKE, Cl. Cur.

p.   Fairfax County Will Book 15th July 1746

170   -The Estate of ROBERT WARDEN Deceased   Dr
        To paid BROWN's Executor
        To paid the Clerk
        To Constable Fees
        To 10 percent for Receiving £1.10.0
        To paid Mr. STURMAN
             Errors Excepted per   WILLIAM HARLE, Exr.
At a Court held for Fairfax County July 15th 1746.
WILLIAM HARLE Executor ROBERT WARDEN deceased exhibited this account against his Estate on oath which is allowed by the Court and admitted to record.
             Test CATESBY COCKE, Cl. Cur.

-Know all men by these presents that we VALINDA WADE, JOHN WEST, WILLIAM WEST and RICHARD SHORE are held and firmly bound unto JOHN COLVILL, Gent. the first Justice in the Commission of the peace for Fairfax County for and in behalf and to the sole use and behoof of the Justices of the said County and their Successors in the sum of one thousand pounds sterling to be paid to the said JOHN COLVILL his Executors Administrators and assigns to the which payment well and truly to be made we bind ourselves and every of us our and every of our heirs Executors and Admrs. jointly and severally firmly by these presents sealed with our seals dated this 15th July 1746.

The Condition of this Obligation is such that if the above bound VALINDA WADE, Admrx. of all the Goods Chattels and Credits of ZEPHANIAH WADE deceased do make or cause to be made a true and perfect Inventory of all and singular the Goods Chattels and Credits of the said Deceased which have or shall come to the hands possession or knowledge of the said VALINDA or unto the hands or possession of any other person or person for her and the

p.   Fairfax County Will Book 15th July 1746

171   same so made do do exhibit or cause to be exhibited into the County Court of Fairfax at such time as she shall be thereto required by the said Court and the same Goods Chattels and Credits and all other the Goods Chattels and Credits of the said Deceased at the time of his death or which at any time after shall come to the hands or possession of the said VALINDA or unto the hands or possession of any other person or persons for her do well and truly administer according to law and further do make a just and true account of her actings and doings therein when thereunto required by the said Court and all the rest and residue of the said Goods Chattels and Credits which shall be found remaining upon the said Admrs. account the same being first examined and allowed by the Justices of the said Court for the time being shall deliver and pay unto such person or persons respectively as the said Justices by their order or judgment shall direct pursuant to the Law in that case made and provided and if it shall hereafter appear that any last Will and Testament was made by the said deceased and the Executor or Executors therein named exhibit the same unto the said Court making request have it allowed and approved accordingly if the said VALINDA being thereunto required do render and deliver up her Letters of Administration approbation of such Testament being first had and made in the said Court. Then this obligation to be void and of none effect or else to remain in full force and vertue.

Sealed and Delivered in presence of   VALINDA V [her mark] WADE [seal]
                                             JOHN WEST [seal]
                                             WILLIAM WEST [seal]
                                             RICHARD SHORE [seal]

At a Court held for Fairfax County July the 15th 1746.

VALINDA WADE, JOHN WEST, WILLIAM WEST and RICHARD SHORE acknowledged this Bond to be their Act and Deed which is admitted to record.

Test   CATESBY COCKE, Clk. Cur.

-Fairfax County, An Inventory of all and singular the Estate of JOHN LITTLETON deceased appraised by us under written appraisers appointed by order of Fairfax

County Court bearing date the 17th of June 1746, we being first sworn before RICHARD OSBORN, Gent. one of his Majesties Justices of the peace for the said County as our hands this 24th July 1746.

19 Hoggs at 5s		£4.15.0
11 Piggs at 1/6		0.16.6

Fairfax County Will Book 19th August 1746

4 cows	£7.0.0	Ditto	0.11.0
2 cows and yearlins at 40s	4.0.0	1 skillet	0.1.0
1 Barren cow	1.10.0	1 flax hackle	0.2.6
3 three year old cattle at 15s	2.5.0	1 set coopers tools	0.10.0
1 steer	1.0.0	A parcel of Carpenters old tools	0.5.0
1 pig	0.1.6	A parcel of axes hoes &c.	0.15.0
1 horse	2.10.0	1 plow and harrow	0.10.0
1 desk	2.0.0	3 chests at 5s	0.15.0
1 bed and covering bedsted and cord	3.10.0	1 Lourn & gear	1.5.0
		1 Linnen wheel	0.10.0
1 ditto	4.0.0	A parcel of lumber	0.10.0
1 ditto	3.0.0	1 saddle	0.7.0
1 pair stilyards	0.7.0	1 bridle harnes & traces	0.1.6
1 box iron and heaters	0.5.0	1 table	0.6.0
1 pair spoon moulds	0.6.0	2 frying pans	0.5.0
1 gun	0.15.0	9# pewter at 1s	3.9.0
1 ditto	0.8.0	2 old coats	0.15.0
1 old crackd pot & hooks	0.4.8		50.4.8
2 potts & 1 pair hooks	0.12.6	5 quart bottles at 3d	0.1.3
		THOMAS LEWIS	£50.5.11
		JAMES HAMILTON } Appraisers	
		JOHN MANLEY	

At a Court held for Fairfax County August 19th 1746.
This Inventory and appraisement of the Estate of JOHN LITTLETON deceased was returned and admitted to record.   Test   CATESBY COCKE, Cl. Cur.

-A true and perfect Inventory and appraisement of all and singular the Estate of Mr. ZEPHANIAH WADE deceased as was presented to our view appraised in current money by us under written appointed by order of Fairfax County Court bearing date the xxth day of July 1746. We being first sworn according to the said Order of appraised the 11th and 12th days of August 1746.
        RICHARD OSBORN, DANIEL FRENCH, JOHN MANLEY

Fairfax County Will Book 19th August 1746
                        Haves

Negro HARRY	35.0.0
Negro GABRIEL	40.0.0
Negro MOLL	30.0.0
Negros SUE and Child named CHARLES	45.0.0
Negro LIDIA	40.0.0

Negro JANE	25.0.0
Negro MOLL a girl	20.0.0.
Negro LUCY a girl	20.0.0
Negro TARY a girl	18.0.0
Negro MURREAH a girl	15.0.0.
Negro PETER a boy	12.0.0.
Indian TOM	40.0.0
White Servants	
THOMAS PEIRCE 1 year & 7 months to serve	5.0.0
MARY SHINBANK 2 years ditto	3.0.0
Cattle	
4 cows and calves at 30s	6.0.0
11 cow at 25s	12.15.0
6 steers at 25s	7.10.0
11 year and 2 year old cattle at 15s	8.5.0
31 sheep at 6s	9.6.0
2 Horses at 4 per 1 Mare ditto 4s	12.0.0
1 old Bay horse	3.0.0
25 sows and barrows young and old swine at 5s	6.5.0
8 ditto at the Mill at 6s	2.8.0
13 ditto at ditto shoals at 20d	1.1.8
13 pigs at ditto at 6d	0.6.6
In the Hall	
1 desk	2.10.0
3 razors at 6d 1 hone 2s	0.3.6
1 pair small money scales and weights	0.5.0
1 wigg 10s 1 ditto 15d	0.11.3
1 spur 4d 1 pair knew buckles 4d 1 per fleams	0.2.8
& 2 lancets 2s	
1 pr. old gloves 6d 1 silver stock buckle 5s	0.5.6
1 pr silver sleeve buttons 18d 1 pr. old silver shoe buckles 7s	0.8.6
1 gum hammer 4d 1 silk purse 18d 1 drumhook 1d	0.1.11
1 Cherrie oval table	0.10.0
1 hempenbelt 18d 1 oval maple table 20s	1.1.6

p.	Fairfax County Will Book 19th August 1746	
174	1 painted table 4s 1 square walnut ditto 10s	0.14.0
	1 shagreen case 11 knifes & 12 forks ivory	1.5.0
	12 old leather chairs at 3/6	2.2.0
	2 old chairs bottm'd with hyde thongs at 6d	0.1.0
	1 pair cast iron doggs	0.10.0
	1 pr. old iron tongs	0.1.0
	1 Looking glass 8s 3 pr. wool cards & old truck 4/6	0.12.6
	1 small Bible	0.4.0
	A parcel of small iron & brass lumber	0.2.6
	A parcel of old books	0.5.0
	3 Decanters at 18d 1 Delph bowl 9d	0.5.3

1 China Bowl 8/ 2 Delph Bowls & 2 Muggs at 2d	0.8.8
1 Liquor Vitie Stand with glass creuits	0.4.0
Old silver weight 13s9d	0.15.9
In the Hall Closet	
Some Delph ware glass	0.2.0
1 old case and bottles 2/ 6 glass bottles	0.3.6
1 Scrubing Brush 6 chest 10s	0.10.6
4 Little Boxes 1 sugar tub	0.2.0
About 6# nails 6# ditto 10# ditto 12s	0.18.0
1 pr. old ditto 1s 2 bells 3s .	0.9.0
In the Hall Chamber	
1 Feather bed 1 bolster 2 pillows 1 blanket 1 old quilt standing bedstead hyde and cord	4.5.0
1 Ditto bed and bolster 2 pillows 1 blanket 1 quilt a walnut truckle bedstead hyde and cord	4.10.0
1 Ditto bed and bolster 1 blanket bedstead hyde and cord	2.10.0
1 seal skin cover	0.10.0
1 small chest	0.3.6
1 old blue cloath close bodied coat	0.8.0
1 suit broad cloath	3.10.0
1 old hat	0.1.3
In the Largest Shed Room	
1 bed and furniture	8.0.0
1 small bed and bolster blankets quilt hyde and cord	2.0.0
1 small oval oak table	0.3.6
1 pair iron doggs 5s 1 looking glass 4d	0.5.4
1 old brushes at 4d 2 stools 4d	0.0.8
In the Small Shed Room	

p. 175	Fairfax County Will Book 19th August 1746	
	1 bed 1 boulster 2 pillows 2 blankets 1 quilt standing bedstead hyde & cord	4.0.0
	1 new bed and bolster	2.0.0
	1 spinning wheel 7/ 1 pr. sheets 10s	0.17.0
	2 suits of curtains at 20s per	2.0.0
	1 brom 6d 2/ pillow beam 16d	0.1.10
	2 pr. old stockings 3/1 warming pan 10s	0.13.0
	1 iron bound box	0.1.0
	3 pair old stockings	0.0.6
	4 pillow bears at 4d 7 towels at 4d	0.3.8
	8 napkins at 6d 3 table cloaths 12/6	0.16.6
	1 skirt 3/ 3 pr. old sheets 10 2 pillow bears at 9d per	0.14.6
	In the Kitchen	
	1 old spinning wheel	0.3.0
	141# old and new pewter at 9d	5.5.9
	1 old saddle 5/ 1 pewter gallon pot 10/	0.15.9
	2 box irons 4 heaters and one old chaffing dish	0.8.0

1 ½ wool at 1s 1 pr. small stilyards 10s	0.11.6
In the Kitchen Loft	
A parcel of Sash Window Glass	0.12.6
1 Chest and 2 earthen panns 5s	0.5.0
About 15# feathers at 1s	0.15.9
6 Bowls at 4d 3 old tubbs at 1s	0.5.0
1x but tan 3s6 1 cradle 5s	0.8.6
1 Beer Cask	0.2.0
In the Kitchen	
1 Table 2s 1 sifters 9d 1 search 18d	0.2.3
2 Tubs 3 pails 2 piggins	0.12.6
1 tray 1s 1 brass kettle 4s	0.5.0
1 Grid Iron 2/6 a parcel old knives and forks at 1	0.3.6
2 Iron spitts at 2/ per	0.4.0
3 Potts at 6per 5 pr. pott hooks at 18d	1.17.6
1 Skillet 2/6 1 pair flesh forks 18d	0.4.0
12 scures and hooks 2/6 25# wool at 1/	1.7.6
1 copper tea kittle 6 s 1 pair snuffers 4d	0.6.4
1 copper coffee pot 4/6	0.4.6
In the Milk Room	
3 brass candle sticks and 1 snuffers	0.4.6
44 pieces of tin ware	0.7.4

p.	Fairfax County Will Book 19th August 1746	
176	1 Table	0.3.0
	21 pieces earthenware 1d per	0.1.9
	2 Tubs at 1d per	0.0.2
	In the Meat House	
	5 old Tubs 4s	0.4.0
	½ Bushels Salt 9d	0.0.9
	1 Butter Potts at 1s 1 bottle Jugg 1s	0.3.0
	1 old Chest and Trifling Lumber	0.2.0
	1 old Tub	0.2.0
	Plantation tools hoes axes ploughs wedges pestle &c	1.0.0
	1 old Cart	0.10.0
	1 Tin garden water bucket	0.2.6
	1 flint glass cruit	0.0.8
	At the Mill	
	1 Coopers ax 6d 1 adze 18d 1 saw 2s	0.4.0
	1 drawing knife 2s 1 half bushel bound 6s	0.8.0
	3 Cast Mill Irons 5s Some iron lumber 18d	0.6.0
	1 frying pan 18d 1 bracket pot 2/6	0.4.0
	1 Servants best clothing	0.10.0
	2 Tobacco hogshead 3/6 13 Tubs at 1/	0.16.6
	2 Mill Pecks & 1 Iron cro 8/ 1 sledge hamer 6d	0.8.6
	4 small mill meusures	0.3.0
	180 shingles 4/8d 443 foot pine plank 5s	1.8.6

A parcel of oider shells about 60 bushels at 2d	0.10.0
35 geese at 1s	1.15.0
20 ducks at 6d	1.13.0
6 old turkeys at 15d	0.7.6
16 young ditto at 7d	<u>0.9.4</u>
VALINDA V [her mark] WADE Admrx.	£493.8.11

At a Court held for Fairfax County August 19th 1746.
This Inventory and appraisement of the Estate of ZEPHANIAH WADE deceased was returned and admitted to record.   Test   CATESBY COCKE, Cl. Cur.

p. <u>Fairfax County Will Book 19th August 1746</u>
177 -With and obedience to and order of Court held June the 17th we being first sworn before WILLIAM PAYNE, Gent. we praise the Estate of JUDITH BALLENGER as followeth

To 1 old cow and calf	2.0.0
To one heifer and calf	1.10.0
To 1 cow yearling	0.15.0
To one old cattail bed and two old blankets and one bolster	0.10.0
To one small new rugg	0.8.0
To one old tartain petticoat and one old pad coat and one	
Old country cloath gound	0.5.0
To one old shift and two old aprons and two old hankshen	0.2.0
To 1 calicoe bonnet and one cap	0.1.0
To one old woting wheel	0.8.0
To one old half bushel and one old bucket	0.0.6
To one old pair of shoes	0.1.0
To one earthen pornger and earthen plait	0.0.4
To 1 pair of old flesh forks and one flat iron	0.0.6
To 1 old frine pan	0.0.6
JOHN IS [his mark] SUMMERS	£6.3.10
WILLIAM M [his mark] BEALE	
JOSEPH COCKERILL	

At a Court held for Fairfax County August 19th 1746.
This Inventory and appraisement of the Estate of JUDITH BALLINGER deceased was returned and admitted to record.   Test   CATESBY COCKE, Clk. Curt.

-We the aforementioned appraisers meat and appraised the remainder part of RICHARD OMOHUNDRA Estate as followeth

To 1 chest at 10s to frying pan at 6d	£0.10.6
To one ovell table	1.0.0
To 1 old chest and a parcel of lumber	0.4.8
To 1 spit and six skures and a driping pan and old box ion	0.9.0
To 1 iron pot at 6s To a Bead and furniture	4.16.0
To one small bedd	1.5.0
To 3 old hoes and a parcell of old lumber	0.4.6
To one pair of cotten cards to one horse and one butten pot	2.12.6
To 1 hoe to a shoemaker hamer	0.3.6

To 1 bull and small beel and one stone jug   1.9.0

p.   <u>Fairfax County Will Book 19th August 1746</u>
178   To 1 mare and colt   1.10.0
   To 1 horse 1.5 To 1 frying pan 2/6   1.7.6
   To 1 old bell and 1 old pessell   <u>0.2.0</u>
       FIELDING TURNER   £15.14.2
       VINCENT LEWIS
       WILLIAM BUCKLEY
At a Court held for Fairfax County August 19th 1746.
This Inventory and appraisment of the Estate of RICHARD OMOHUMDRA deceased
was returned and admitted to record.   Test CATESBY COCKE, Cl. Cur.

-In Obedience to an order of Fairfax County Court dated 20th May we the
subscribers being first sworn before JOHN WEST, Gent. did meat and appraise the
Estate of JOHN CRUMPTON deceased Vizt.
   To 3 Cows and calves at 10d per piece   4.10.0
   To 4 yearlings at 7/6 per piece   1.10.0
   To 1 mare and colt 1.5 to 1 old mare 5s   1.10.0
   To 1 old horse 10s to 11 heads of sheet at 5s per piece   4.0.0
   To 14 head of geas at 19d   0.10.6
   To 7 heads of hogs and 6/6 per piece 1.11.6 to 7 shoats at 2s   2.5.6
   To 1 pint bottles at 2d to a parcel of earthenware 2s   0.12.6
   To a parcel of old iron lumber 15s to a parcel of old tubs 2/6   0.17.6
   To a masking tab half bushel pail and 2 old pigins   0.5.0
   To 3 old spinning wheels 5 to 1 old gun 5s   0.10.0
   To 3 old meal sifters and 2 wheat sives   0.7.6
   To 1 Lantren 1 lamp 1 box iron and some lumber   0.10.0
   To 1 sadle and bridle 10s To a parcel of tin ware 5s   0.15.0
   To 2 old chests and 3 old boxes 5s 1 old chafen dish 1/6   0.6.6
   To his wareing apparrel   1.15.0
   To 2 old tables and 4 old chairs 2/6 to 2 frying pans   0.5.6
   To 4 potts and 3 pr. pott hooks 20s To 6 old books 3s   1.3.0
   To 2 old baggs 1/ To 4 old knives and forks 9d to 1 pr. tongs
     And flesh forks 2s   0.3.9
   To 1 old Bead and Covering 1.5 to 1 bead and covering 2.10   3.15.0

p.   <u>Fairfax County Will Book 19th August 1746</u>
179   To 1 old flock bead and covering 10s To 1 old bead quilt 5s   0.15.0
   To 1 old beadstead Hyde and cord 5s to 2 old trundle beadsteads   0.11.0
   To 11# Woll at 9d 8/3 To 38# putter at 9d 1.8.9   1.17.0
   To 1 hearing neat   0.1.6
       JOHN TAYLOR   £28.16.9
       GILBERT SIMPSON
       SAMPSON DARRELL
At a Court held for Fairfax County August 19th 1746.

This Inventory and appraisment of the Estate of JOHN CRUMPTON deceased was returned and admitted to record.   Test   CATESBY COCKE, Cl. Cur.

-Fairfax   We the Subscribers whose names are under written being first sworn have praised and valued all the Estate of ELIAS MITCHELL deceased as came to our view &c.

1 Bagg and one wig and 2 pair of traces	0.9.6
2 Checkd shirts and 2 jacketts	0.7.6
1 razor and 1 pair of clasps	0.2.0
1 Saddle and old trunk	0.2.0
1 pair of leather breeches and hat	0.2.6
1 pair of stockings and an old coat	0.4.6
1 runlet and lumber and old tub	0.4.6
To Beens	0.4.6
To 150# beaff	0.18.10 1/2
To 6 barrels of corn	2.8.0
To 6 heens and 1 cock	0.3.6
To 9# of beaff	0.1.1 1/2
To 1 book 1s 1 gun 16s	0.17.0
To 1 old tub	0.1.6
PHILIP NOLAND	£6.4.0

JOHN O [his mark] GIBSON
WILLIAM HALLINGE

At a Court continued and held for Fairfax County August 20th 1746.
This Inventory and appraisment of the Estate of ELIAS MITCHELL deceased was returned and admitted to record.   Test   CATESBY COCKE, Cl. Cur.

p.   Fairfax County Will Book 16th September 1746
180   -A True Inventory of the Estate of HENRY OKEAN, To the Worshipfull his Majesties Justices of Fairfax County, We your humble servant. In Obedience to your Worships order have appraised all and singular the Estate of HENRY OKEAN as was brought to our sight.

JOHN IS [his mark] SUMMERS, WILLIAM O [his mark] DAVEY, JOHN EVANS

To one negro man named JACK	£35.0.0
To one negro mane named GAWASH	35.0.0
To one negro woman named RACHEL	35.0.0
To 17 hogs about a year old	4.0.0
To 35 shoats and pigs	4.15.0
To 3 cows and calves	5.5.0
To 1 old sow and a yearlin	1.15.0
To 2 2 year old steers	1.10.0
To 2 yearlin steers	1.0.0
To 2 2 year old heifers	1.5.0
To 1 small grey horse	3.0.0
To 1 old horse and a old saddle and bridle	4.0.0
To a small horse	8.0.0
To one feather bed bedstead and furniture	6.10.0

To one feather bed trunnel bedstead furniture	4.10.0
To 7 pewter dishes	1.9.0
To 14 pewter plates	0.15.0
To 16 spoons	0.3.0
To a pewter basons	0.8.0
To 1 pewter tanket	0.2.0
To 2 old tin pans	0.1.0
To 2 old jackets and a old pair of breeches	0.12.0
To 1 old great coat and an old jacket	0.5.0
To 1 broad cloath coat and a marrowbroad cloath jacket	2.10.0
To 2 old chests and 2 old boxes	0.10.0
To 2 old tables and 4 old chairs	0.7.0
To 2 old wooden stools	0.1.6
To 2 very old guns	2.5.0
To 11 knives and 15 forks	0.5.0
To 1 iron pot	0.10.0
To 1 small old frying pan sadle and flesh fork	0.3.0
To 4 old water pails	0.5.0
To 4 old axes	0.3.0

p.
181

Fairfax County Will Book 16th September 1746

To one ax	0.4.0
To 3 iron wedges	0.5.0
To 1 drawing knife and a hamber	0.2.0
To 1 iron gredle	0.2.0
To a parcel of old hoes	0.5.0
To 6 sickels	0.3.0
To 1 old sauce pan	0.0.6
To 2 pair of pot hooks	0.2.0
To 1 old Riddle and a Tray and 19 Glass bottles	0.5.0
To 1 earthen judg	0.0.6
To 1 small runlet	0.1.6
To 1 old churn	0.2.0
To 1 rasor and hone a pair of spoon moles &c	0.5.6
JENNY OKEAN Exrx.	£64.2.6

At a Court held for Fairfax County September 16th 1746.
This Inventory and appraisement of the Estate of HENRY OKEAN deceased was returned and admitted to record.   Test   CATESBY COCKE, Cl. Cur.

-Know all men by these presents that we JOHN STURMAN & BENJAMIN SEBASTIAN are held and firmly bound unto JOHN COLVILL, Gent. first Justice in the Commission of the peace for Fairfax County for and in behalf and to the sole use and behoof of the Justices of the said County and their Successors In the sum of fifty pounds sterling To be paid to the said JOHN COLVILL his Executors Admrs. and assigns to the which payment well and truly to be made we bind ourselves and every of us our and every of our heirs Executors and Admrs. jointly and severally firmly by these presents sealed with our seals dated this 16th day of September 1746.

The Condition of this Obligation is such that if the above bound JOHN STURMAN Admr. of all the Goods Chattels and Credits of WILLIAM STURMAN deceased do make or cause to be made a true and perfect Inventory of all and singular the Goods Chattels and Credits of the said deceased have or shall come to the hands possession or knowledge of the said JOHN or unto the hands or possession of any other person or persons for him and the same so made, do exhibit or cause to be exhibited into the County Court of Fairfax at such time a she shall be thereto required by the said Court, and the same Goods Chattels and Credits and all other the Goods

p.   Fairfax County Will Book 16th September 1746
181   Chattels and Credits of the said deceased at the time of his death or which at
        any time after shall come to the hands or possession of the said JOHN or unto
the hands or possession of any other person or persons for him do well and truly administer according to Law and further do make a just and true account of his actings and doings therein when thereto required by the said Court, and all the rest and residue of the said Goods Chattels and Credits which shall be found remaining upon the said Adms. account the same being first examined and allowed by the Justices of the said County for the time being shall deliver and pay unto such person or persons respectively as the said Justices by their order or Judgment shall direct pursuant to the Law in that case made and provided, and if it shall hereafter appear that any last Will and Testament was made by the said deceased, And the Executor Executors therein named do exhibit the same into the said Court making request to have it allowed and approved accordingly the said JOHN being thereunto required do render and deliver his Letters of Administration approbation of such Testament being first had and made in the said Court, Then this obligation to be void else to remain in full force and vertue.
        Sealed and Delivered in the presence of   JOHN STURMAN [seal]
                                                    BENJAMIN SEBASTIAN [seal]
At a Court held for Fairfax County September 16th 1746.
JOHN STURMAN & BENJAMIN SEBASTIAN, Gent. acknowledged this Bond to be their Act and Deed which is admitted to record. Test   CATESBY COCKE, Cl. Cur.

        -In the name of God Amen the 1st of October in the year of our Lord God 1744. JOHN MUSGROVE in the County of Fairfax Gent. being very sick and weak in body but of perfect mind and memory thanks be given unto God therefore calling to mind the morality of my body and knowing that it is appointed for all men once to die, do make and ordain this my last Will and Testament, that is to say, principally and first of all I give and recommend my soul into the hands of God that gave it and or my body I commend it to the Earth to be buried in a Christian like and decent manner

p.   Fairfax County Will Book 17th September 1746
182   at the discretion of my Executors, nothing dobling but at the General
        Resurrection I shall receive the same again by the mighty power of God and as
touched & such worldly Estate wherewith it hath pleased God to bless me in the life I give devise and dispose of the same in the following manner and form.
Imprimis I give and bequeath to my well beloved son EDWARD MUSGROVE my dwelling plantation that I now live on and all my stock hogs cattle horses with all my

furniture belonging to the said Plantation Tables Chests beds and bed cloaths puter pots and pans with all and every article belonging to the said plantation likewise I do will and give him that plantation which HENRY BRENT has rented of me with all my lands and houses in Maryland and one negro fellow called DICK.

Item I do give to my beloved son JOHN MUSGROVE that Plantation that JOSEPH HUNT lives upon with all things belonging thereunto and one Negro boy called TOM and his horse saddle and bridle.

Item I do give to my son WILLIAM MUSGROVE all that tract of land that is now in dispute with one negro boy called GEORGE with half that tract of land that I had of WILLIAM SEA with two mare.

Item I give to my son CULBERT MUSGROVE that plantation called WILSON's with that Plantation upon Sherindo River that I have of WILLIAM SEA and JOSEPH KING with half the tract and half the stock of cattle hogs and horses with his riding horse Shaver.

I give to my well beloved daughter MARY MUSGROVE that Plantation that is now held by JEREMIAH SPURLING with all things appertaining thereunto with one negro man called HANNAH with her horse saddle and bridle.

I give to my well beloved daughter ANN MOSLEY my quarter that is now in being with half that tract of land which I bought of JAMES BAUL and one negro garil called JUDY and two cows big with caulf ten head of hogs two ewes big with young with one grey horse and two horses.

Item I give to my daughter MARGRET MUSGROVE that Plantation and land that JAMES BOLTON lives on with two hundred acres of land upon Sherindo River near to the ford with the Benefit of half the stock belonging to the said Plantation to be divided between her and her sister MARY with all my lands upon Sherindo river that is not mentioned upon clearing the Deeds share and share alike amongst all my children.

I do likewise will that all the Tobacco and all the Rents which is now in the houses shall go to pay all my and my children's debts and if there is not enough to pay what is due this year, then all the Rents with the Crop which is made the year following shall go to pay the remainder of the

p.   Fairfax County Will Book 17th September 1746
184   debt and what remains of the Crop and the Rents to be Equally divided amongst my seven children.

I do likewise give all my young horses mares and colts to my son JOHN and DONALD MOXLEY to be divided between them as they think fit running upon the back Lick.

Item I do give to JOHN BOLTEN son of JAMES BOLTEN two young sows and one large young bay mare big with colt that was branded by JOHN HOLLISES son.

I do likewise Institute my son EDWARD and my son is Law DONALD MOXLEY to be my Executors to see all my debts carefully paid and to see that all my children have their just due and right and that my children shall be free.

And this is my last Will and Testament and I do hereby utterly disallow revoke and disannul all and every other former Testaments Wills Legacies Requests by me anyways before this time named Wills and bequeath ratifying and confirming this and no other to be my last Will and Testament. In Witness whereof I have hereunto set my hand and seal the day and year first above written.

Signed Sealed published pronounced & declared by the said as his last Will
and Testament in the presence of us the subscribers
JOHN DAYSON, WILLIAM X [his mark] MOXLEY [seal]
JEREMIAH X [his mark] SPARKS, JAME X [her mark] MOXLEY
WILLIAM P [his mark] PARSONS   JOHN MUSGROVE [seal]
At a Court continued and held for Fairfax County September 17th 1746.
This last Will and Testament of JOHN MUSGROVE deceased was presented in Court
by EDWARD MUSGROVE one of the Executors therein named, DANIEL MOXLEY the
other Executor having Relinquished his Executorship, who made oath thereto
according to Law and the same is proved by WILLIAM MOXLEY, JEREMIAH SPARKS &
JANE MOXLEY and admitted to record, and on motion of the said Executor and his
performing what is usual in such cases Certificate is granted him for obtaining a
probate in due form.   Test   CATESBY COCKE, Cl. Cur.

p.   Fairfax County Will Book 17th September 1746
185   -Pursuant to an order of Fairfax County Court dated the 20th May 1746. We
        the subscribers being sworn before EDWARD BARRY, Gent. have Inventory'd
all and singular the Estate of DAVID BATHENS Estate which came to view. Vizt.

Looking Glass	0.1.6
Iron Skillet	0.2.0
One ditto	0.1.6
Pot Wrack	0.5.0
Earthen pot	0.0.1
Spit	0.2.0
Candle stick 6d pothooks	0.2.6
Iron pot and hooks	0.2.6
	£0.17.1

WILLIAM BRONAUGH & ELIZABETH BRONAUGH, Admrs.   WILLIAM CHAMPNEYS
                                                 WILLIAM READON
                                                 THOMAS ANDERSON
At a Court continued and held for Fairfax County September 17th 1746.
This Inventory and appraisement of the Estate of DANIEL BETHEL deceased was
returned and admitted to record.   Test   CATESBY COCKE, Cl. Cur.

        -In the name of God Amen. I ROBERT BOLING of Truro pairsh Fairfax County in
the Colony of Virginia planter being sick and weak of body but of perfect mind and
memory thanks be to God, do publish and declare this my last Will and Testament,
first I commend my soul to the hands of Almighty God hoping through my Savior
Jesus Christ to use again from the dead and my body to the ground to be decently
bered at the descretion of my Executrix under nominated and appointed.
Item I give to my beloved wife MARY BOLING the same forth part of my lands during
her natural life and the forth part of my personal Estate.
Item I give and bequeath to my Cozen SIMON BOLING fifty acres of land to him and
the heirs of his body and in case of no lawful heirs to return to my heirs again.
Item I give and bequeath that my Cozen ROBERT BOLING should have an equal part
with my children and in case he should have no heirs to return to my heirs again.

Item I give and bequeath to my wifes daughter ELIZABETH BOLING and MARTHA BOLING should have their equal parts in my Estate when my Cosen ROBERT BOLING comes to the age of twenty one years to be delivered to him and my wifes daughter ELIZABETH and MARTHA when they come to the age of sixteen years to be delivered unto them.

Item I nominate and appoint MARY BOLING my beloved wife to be my

p.   Fairfax County Will Book 17th September 1746
186   whole and sole Executrix of all my personal Estate Virs. of all Goods Chattels
         Lands and Tenements &c. revoking all other Testaments or Wills by me
formerly made in witness whereof I have hereunto put my hand and seal this thirty first day of March in the year of our Lord 1746.

                                         ROBERT RB [his mark] BOLING [seal]
         Signed Sealed and published in presence of
                  TOWNSHEND DADE, JOSEPH X [his mark] BOLING, J. WYBIRD
At a Court continued and held for Fairfax County September 17th 1746.
This last Will and Testament of ROBERT BOLING deceased was presented in Court by MARY BOLING who relinquishes the Executorship and on her motion and performing what is usual in such cases Certificate is granted her for obtaining Letters of Administration with the said Will Annexed in due form.
                  Test   CATESBY COCKE, Cl. Cur.

         -Know all men by these presents that we MARY BOLING, JOHN EVANS and WILLIAM DAVIE are held and firmly bound unto JOHN COLVILL, Gent. first Justice in the Commission of the peace for Fairfax County for and in behalf and to the sole use and behoof of the Justices of the said County and their Successors in the sum of two hundred pounds sterling To be paid to the said JOHN COLVILL his Executors Admrs. and assigns to the which payment well and truly to be made we bind ourselves and every of us our and every of our heirs Executors and Admrs. jointly and severally firmly by these presents sealed with our seals dated this 17th day of September 1746.
The Condition of this Obligation is such that if the above bound MARY BOLING, Admrx. with the last Will and Testament of ROBERT BOLING deceased thereunto annexed do make or cause to be made a true and perfect Inventory of all and singular the Goods Chattels and Credits of the said deceased have or shall come to the hands possession or knowledge of the said JOHN or unto the hands or possession of any other person or persons for him and the same so made, do exhibit or cause to be exhibited into the County Court of Fairfax at such time as she shall be thereto required by the said Court, and the same Goods Chattels and Credits and all other the Goods Chattels and Credits of the said deceased at the time of his death or which at any time after shall

p.   Fairfax County Will Book 17th September 1746
187   come to the hands or possession of the said MARY or unto the hands or
         possession of any other person or persons for her do well and truly administer
according to Law and further do make a just and true account of their actings and doings therein when thereunto required by the Court, And also do well and truly pay

and deliver all the Legacies contained and specified in the said Testament as far as the said Goods Chattels and Credits will therewith extend and the Law shall charge her then this obligation to be void and of none effect or else to remain in full force and vertue.   Signed and Delivered in presence of

> MARY = [her mark] BOLING [seal]
> JOHN EVANS [seal]
> WILLIAM O [her mark] DAVIE [seal]

At a Court continued and held for Fairfax County September 17th 1746.
MARY BOLING, JOHN EVANS & WILLIAM DAVIE acknowledged this Bond to be their Act and deed which is admitted to record. Test   CATESBY COCKE, Cl. Cur.

-Know all Men by these presents that We HENRY TREN & JAMES HAMILTON are held and firmly bound unto JOHN COLVILL, Gent. first Justice in the Commission of the peace for Fairfax County for and in behalf and to the sole use and behoof of the Justices of the said County and their Successors in the sum of two hundred pounds sterling To be paid to the said JOHN COLVILL his Executors Admrs. and assigns to the which payment well and truly to be made we bind ourselves and every of us our and every of our heirs Executors and Admrs. jointly and severally firmly by these presents sealed with our seals dated this 21st day of October 1746.
The Condition of this Obligation is such that if the above bound HENRY TREN Admr. of all the Goods Chattels and Credits of WILLIAM BURSTON deceased do make or cause to be made a true and perfect Inventory of all and singular the Goods Chattels and Credits of the said deceased which have or shall come to the hands possession or knowledge of the said HENRY do unto the hands or possession of any other person or persons for him, and the same so made do exhibit or cause to be exhibited into the County Court of Fairfax at such time as he shall be thereto required by the said Court and the same Goods Chattels and Credits and all other the Goods Chattels and Credits of the said deceased at the time of his death or which at any time shall come to the hands or possession of the said HENRY or unto the hands or possession of any other person or

p.   Fairfax County Will Book 20th October 1746
188   persons for him do well and truly administer according to law and further do make a just and true account of his actings and doings therein when hereto required by the said Court, and all the Rest and residue of the said Goods Chattels and Credits which shall be found remaining upon the said Admrs. account the same being first examined and allowed by the Justices of the said Court for the time being shall deliver and pay unto such person or persons respectively as the said Justices by their order or judgment shall direct pursuant to the Law in that Case made and provided, And if it shall hereafter appear that any last Will and Testament was made by the said deceased and the Executor or Exrs. therein named do exhibit the same unto the said Court making request to have it allowed and approved accordingly the said HENRY being thereunto required to render and deliver up his Letters of Administration approbation of such Testament being first had and made in the said Court Then the Obligation to be void else to remain in full force and vertue.
    Sealed and Delivered in the presence of us

> HENRY IT [his mark] TREN [seal]   JAMES HAMILTON [seal]

At a Court held for Fairfax County October 20th 1746.
HENRY TREN & JAMES HAMILTON acknowledged this Bond to be their Act and Deed which is admitted to record.　　　　Test CATESBY COCKE, Cl. Cur.

-We the Subscribers being first sworn before a Justice of the peace for Fairfax County did value and appraise the Estate of WILLIAM STURMAN deceased as follows

1 young bay mare	£1.10.0
1 mare and colt	1.5.0
1 bed and furniture	3.10.0
2 wigs	1.5.0
1 fiddle	0.12.6
1 gun	1.0.0
To his wareing apparel	7.0.0
1 silk purse 1 pair money seals 2 pair sleeve buttons and some awls	0.6.3
1 Gold ring	0.12.0
1 pair of pumps	0.4.0
	£18.19.9

p.　　Fairfax County Will Book 18th November 1746
189　　　　　　　　　　ROBERT BOGGESS
　　　　　　　　　　THOMAS MOXLEY
　　　　　　　　　　JOHN APPLETON　　　JOHN STURMAN, Admr.
At a Court held for Fairfax County November 18th 1746.
This Inventory and appraisement of the Estate of WILLIAM STURMAN deceased was returned and admitted to record.　　Test　CATESBY COCKE, Cl. Cur.

-In Obedience to an order of Fairfax Court dated the 17th of September 1746. We the Subscribers met and being first sworn valued the Estate of ROBERT BOLING deceased as followeth Vizt.

To 3 cows and calves	4.10.0
To 2 steers	3.0.0
To 9 heifers	1.10.0
To 1 yearling	0.10.0
To eight large shoats at 5s	2.0.0
To 3 spay'd sows	1.4.0
To seventeen small shoats	2.2.6
To two breeding sows	0.19.0
To a bear	0.5.0
To an old mare and colt	4.0.0
To an white horse	0.3.0
To three horse bells	0.12.0
To a bed bolster rug blanket bed sted and hide	2.10.0
To one ditto	2.15.0
To 2 old chests	0.10.0
To a spining wheel	0.5.0
To 4 old chairs and one old table	0.8.0

To Philadelphia saddle	1.5.0
To one old ditto	0.5.0
To an old gun	0.8.0
To small looking glass	0.1.0
To two mugs and two porringers a drinking glass	0.1.8
To 3 pair of old wool cards	0.5.0
To parcel of iron work	1.5.0

p.   Fairfax County Will Book 18th November 1746

190	To a parcel of Coopers Tools	£0.5.0
	To a parcel of old iron	0.7.6
	To a parcel of iron work	0.7.0
	To a small parcel of powder and lead	0.0.4
	To a parcel of earthenware	0.7.0
	To a parcel quart bottles	0.3.0
	To a parcel old tubs	0.10.0
	To a parcel old feathers	0.3.0
	To a parcel old pewter	0.8.0
	To a pewter can and funnel 2 old basons	0.6.0
	To 2 iron froes	0.5.0
	To pair hamrs and traces and piece old roap	0.1.0
	To pair small sheers and a parcel old knives and forks	0.1.6
	To an old bedstid 3 old sifters one old book	0.2.6
	To an old rug and an old bag	0.2.0
	To 3 old tubs and 2 piggins	0.3.0
	To 3 baskets and tray and a hamper	0.2.0
	To three old iron pots and 2 pair pothooks a frying pan	0.12.0
	To 3 bells strap and pair of hobbles	0.1.6
	To 19 head of sheep	5.8.0
	To a small grinding stone	0.1.0

TOWNSHEND DADE   £40.3.6
JOHN GLADIN
JOHN V [his mark] STRAUGHAN

At a Court held for Fairfax County November 18th 1746.
This Inventory and appraisement of the Estate of ROBERT BOLING deceased was returned and admitted to record.   Test   CATESBY COCKE, Cl. Cur.

-Know all men by these presents that we EDWARD EMMS, JAMES JENKINS and JOHN LUCAS are held and firmly bound unto JOHN COLVILL, Gent. first Justice in the Commission of the peace for Fairfax County for and in behalf and to the sole use and behoof of the Justices of the said County and their Successors in the sum of one hundred pounds sterling to be paid to the said JOHN COLVILL his Executors Admrs. and assigns to the which

p.   Fairfax County Will Book 18th November 1746

191   payment well and truly to be made we bind ourselves and every of us our and every of our heirs Executors and Admrs. jointly and severally firmly by these

presents sealed with our seals dated this 18th day of November 1746.
The Condition of this Obligation is such that if the above bound EDWARD EMMS,
Admr. of all the Goods Chattels and Credits of LYDIA NEALE deceased do make or
cause to be made a true and perfect Inventory of all and singular the Goods Chattels
and Credits of the said deceased which have or shall come to the hands possession
or knowledge of the said EDWARD do unto the hands or possession of any other
person or persons for him, and the same so made do exhibit or cause to be exhibited
into the County Court of Fairfax at such time as he shall be thereto required by the
said Court and the same Goods Chattels and Credits and all other the Goods Chattels
and Credits of the said deceased at the time of his death or which at any time shall
come to the hands or possession of the said EDWARD or unto the hands or
possession of any other person or persons for him do well and truly administer
according to law and further do make a just and true account of his actings and
doings therein when hereto required by the said Court and all the rest and residue of
the said Goods Chattels and Credits which shall be found remaining upon the said
Admrs. account the same being first examined and allowed by the Justices of the
said Court for the time being shall deliver and pay unto such person or persons
respectively as the said Justices by their order or judgment shall direct pursuant to
the Law in that Case made and provided, And if it shall hereafter appear that any last
Will and Testament was made by the said deceased and the Executor or Exrs. therein
named do exhibit the same unto the said Court making request to have it allowed
and approved accordingly the said EDWARD being thereunto required to render and
deliver up his Letters of Administration approbation of such Testament being first had
and made in the said Court then the Obligation to be void else to remain in full force
and vertue.

Sealed and Delivered in the presence of   EDWARD E [his mark] EMMS [seal]
JAMES X [his mark] JENKINS [seal]{
JOHN LUCAS [seal]

At a Court held for Fairfax County November 18th 1746.
EDWARD EMMS, JAMES JENKINS and JOHN LUCAS acknowledged this Bond to be
their Act and Deed which is admitted to record.   Test   CATESBY COCKE, Cl. Cur.

p.   Fairfax County Will Book 17th March 1746/7
192   -An Additional inventory of Maj. McCARTY deceased which came to hand after
the appraisment.
One Negro THAD and her child GEORGE
SARAH McCARTY
At a Court held for Fairfax County March 17th 1746.
This additional Inventory of the Estate of DENIS McCARTY, Gent. deced. was returned
and ordered to be recorded.   Test   CATESBY COCKE, Cl. Cur.

-Dr   The Estate of Maj. McCARTY, Deced.   Contra   Cr.
To Mrs. SARAH McCARTY widow 17 negros By the total of Inventory 1441.2.8
To DANIEL McCARTY 7 Ditto
To SARAH McCARTY 7 ditto
To ANN McCARTY 7 ditto
To DENIS McCARTY 6 ditto

To THADDEUS McCARTY 7 ditto   1144.0.0
To Mrs. McCARTY 3d part of stock and goods 93.10.4 ½
To DANIEL McCARTY Legacy & 15 p ditto 75.11.5 1/2
To SARAH McCARTY, Jun. 15 per ditto 30.14.9 3/4
To ANN McCARTY 15 per ditto 30.14.9 3/4
To DENIS McCARTY 15 per ditto 30.14.9 3/4
To THADDEUS McCARTY 15 per ditto 30.14.9 ¾
To mistakes in Inventory   5.1.7
                                  £1441.2.8   £1441.2.8

Fairfax Pursuant to an order of Court to us directed to value and set the proportional part of the estate of DENIS McCARTY, Gent. deceased between SARAH McCARTY relict of the said DENIS & DANIEL McCARTY, SARAH McCARTY, Jun. & ANN McCARTY children to the said DENIS minors not mentioned in the said order We did on the date hereof value and set apart the said estate according to the will of the said DENIS deceased and the Inventory in manner following.

To the relict the following slaves SAM, RODHAM, SAWRY or JACK, STAFFORD, ALICE, HANNAH, MARIA, SARAH, DREW, MINEY, JUDY, NANCY, BOB, BOB, GEORGE, WILLOBY, FREDRICK & one third part of the Chattels amounting to ninety pounds ten shillings and four pence half penny.

p.   Fairfax County Will Book 17th March 1746/7
193   To Mr. DANIEL McCARTY, the following slaves GEORGE, FREDRICK, NAN,
       LETTICE, SARAH, PHILL, WILL and one fifth part of the Chattels amounting to
thirty pounds fourteen shillings nine pence three farthings exclusive of Legacies.
To SARAH McCARTY, Jun. the following slaves SENGO, MARGARET, JACK, SABRINA YOUNG, SONGO, JOAN, MARY & YOUNG SABRINA and one fifth part of the Chattels amounting to thirty pounds fourteen shillings and nine pence three farthings.
To ANN McCARTY the following slaves PETER, MULATTO PETER, BLACK PETER, BESS FIRE, WINNY, MARY and one fifth part of the Chattels amounting to thirty pounds fourteen shillings and nine pence three farthings.
To DENIS McCARTY the following slaves THAD, MOL, MAURER, DUKE, KING and fifteen pounds current money for the value of his part of a negro child to be paid DANIEL, SARAH, ANN & THADDEUS unto DENIS McCARTY there parts and one third part of the Chattels amounting to thirty pounds fourteen shillings nine pence three farthings.
To THADDEUS the following slaves LONDON, SAM, LUCY, BECK, MARIA, BESS, GEORGE and one fifth part of the Chattels amounting to thirty pounds fourteen shillings nine pence three farthings which division may more fully and distinctly appear by an amount therein given under our hands this Second October 1745.
NB the slaves and proportional part of this estate and JOHN WEST belonging to DENIS & THADDEUS McCARTY Administrators.
At a Court held for Fairfax County March 17th 1746.
This Division of the estate of DENIS McCARTY, Gent. deceased was returned and admitted to record.   Test   CATESBY COCKE, Cl. Curt.

    -Know all men by these presents that we JOHN NORTH & LAWRENCE WASHINGTON are held and firmly and firmly bound unto JOHN COLVILL, Gent. first

Justice in the Commission of the peace for Fairfax County for and in behalf and to the sole use and behoof of the Justices of the said County and their Successors in the sum of two hundred pounds sterling to be paid to the said JOHN COLVILL his Executors Admrs. and assigns to the which payment well and truly to be made we bind ourselves and every of us our and every of our heirs Executors and Admrs. jointly and severally firmly by these presents sealed with our seals dated this 17th day of March 1746.
The Condition of this Obligation is such that if the above bound JOHN NORTH administrator of all the Goods Chattels and Credits of WILLIAM GRIMWOOD deceased

p.   Fairfax County Will Book 17th March 1746/7
194   do make or cause to be made a true and perfect Inventory of all and singular the Goods Chattels and Credits of the said deceased which have or shall come to the hands possession or knowledge of the said JOHN do unto the hands or possession of any other person or persons for him, and the same so made do exhibit or cause to be exhibited into the County Court of Fairfax at such time as he shall be thereto required by the said Court and the same Goods Chattels and Credits and all other the Goods Chattels and Credits of the said deceased at the time of his death or which at any time shall come to the hands or possession of the said JOHN or unto the hands or possession of any other person or persons for him do well and truly administer according to law and further do make a just and true account of his actings and doings therein when hereto required by the said Court and all the rest and residue of the said Goods Chattels and Credits which shall be found remaining upon the said Admrs. account the same being first examined and allowed by the Justices of the said Court for the time being shall deliver and pay unto such person or persons respectively as the said Justices by their order or judgment shall direct pursuant to the Law in that Case made and provided, And if it shall hereafter appear that any last Will and Testament was made by the said deceased and the Executor or Exrs. therein named do exhibit the same unto the said Court making request to have it allowed and approved accordingly the said JOHN being thereunto required to render and deliver up his Letters of Administration approbation of such Testament being first had and made in the said Court Then the Obligation to be void else to remain in full force and vertue.
Sealed and Delivered in presence of   JOHN NORTH [seal]
                                        LAWRENCE WASHINGTON [seal]
At a Court held for Fairfax County March 17th 1746/7
JOHN NORTH and LAWRENCE WASHINGTON, Gent. acknowledged this Bond to be their Act and Deed which is admitted to record.   Test   CATESBY COCKE, Cl. Cur.

-Pursuant to an order of Fairfax Court dated the 17th September 1746. We the Subscribers met at the house of ROBERT BOLING deceased and valued the remainder of his estate as followeth.   £.S.D
        To one bay mare   1.15.0
        To two young steers   2.0.0

p.   Fairfax County Will Book 17th March 1746/7
195   To an old broad ax   0.3.0

To a gun lock an old razor and a wooden tray	0.4.0
To a pair spoon moulds and a fluke plow	<u>0.11.0</u>
The 6th of February 1746/7	£4.13.0

TOWNSHEND DADE

JOHN GLADIN

JOHN E [his mark] STRAUGHAN

At a Court held for Fairfax County March 17th 1746.
This additional Inventory and appraisment of the estate of ROBERT BOLING deceased was returned and admitted to record.   Test   CATESBY COCKE, Cl. Cur.

-An Inventory of all and singular the estate of WILLIAM BURSTON deceased appraised by us under written being sworn before one of his Majesties Justices according to order of Fairfax County Court bearing date the 21st October 1746 appraised 25th day of October 1740. RICHARD OSBORN

1 feather bed bolster	3.0.0
1 at 2/6 Dittto at 2/4 ditto	1.2.0
2 Drawing knives	0.4.0
3 Foot adzes at 20# percent	1.0.0
1 [unreadable]	0.1.3
1 [unreadable]	0.7.0
1 broken foot adze	0.1.6
1 saw	0.5.0
1 stone	0.14.0
1 saws 8s 1 box iron & pestle	0.13.0
2 [unreadable]	0.0.0
1 cow and calf 1 heifer	3.0.0
1 old horse	1.10.0
A parcel of small pails of iron lumber and basket	0.12.0
5# lead 2 old spoons 2d 2 pot iron at 3d	0.7.3
1 plow iron and colter 2 broad hoes at 2/cent	0.9.0
3 arrow hoes at 4d cent marrow ax at 2/6	0.3.0
1 old broad ax 6d feather bad bridle and rope 18d	0.2.0
1 Table form and stool 18d 5 old tubs	0.2.6
2 pails rund lot and small sood bowl	0.4.5
3 Glass bottles at 2d percent	0.0.6
Sundry Trifles in a box old knives fork and sisars and buttons	0.6.0
1 sifter and trowel 1s2 old linnen bags 1s	0.2.0
1 Chest and old cloths 36s7 yard kersey at 3s	2.19.0
A parcel of damaged corn	0.10.0
1 frying pan 1 iron wedge 1 rasp hatchet	0.3.0

p.
196

<u>Fairfax County Will Book 17th March 1746/7</u>

1 heifer 18s	0.18.0
3 Barrows at 6/6d 3 sows at 5/63 shoats at 4 ½ d	0.9.0
16 pigs at 10d 1 pair compasses 1s	0.14.0
2 iron hoops at 1/per	0.2.0

1 cart sadle collar and harns   0.2.0
                    HENRY HT[his mark] TREN, Admr.
At a Court held for Fairfax County March 17th 1746.
This Inventory and appraisement of the estate of WILLIAM BURSTON
deceased was returned and admitted to record.
                    Test   CATESBY COCKE, Cl. Cur.

-Know all these men by these presents that we WILLIAM JANNEY & JOHN
EVANS are held and firmly bound unto JOHN COLVILL, Gent. first Justice in the
Commission of the peace for Fairfax County for and in behalf and to the sole use and
behoof of the Justices of the said County and their Successors in the sum of four
hundred pounds sterling to be paid to the said JOHN COLVILL his Executors Admrs.
and assigns to the which payment well and truly to be made we bind ourselves and
every of us our and every of our heirs Executors and Admrs. jointly and severally
firmly by these presents sealed with our seals dated this 17th day of March 1746.
The Condition of this Obligation is such that if the above bound WILLIAM JANNEY
Admr. of all the Goods Chattels and Credits of MARK THOMAS deceased do make or
cause to be made a true and perfect Inventory of all and singular the Goods Chattels
and Credits of the said deceased which have or shall come to the hands possession
or knowledge of the said WILLIAM do unto the hands or possession of any other
person or persons for him, and the same so made do exhibit or cause to be exhibited
into the County Court of Fairfax at such time as he shall be thereto required by the
said Court and the same Goods Chattels and Credits and all other the Goods Chattels
and Credits of the said deceased at the time of his death or which at any time shall
come to the hands or possession of the said WILLIAM or unto the hands or
possession of any other person or persons for him do well and truly administer
according to law and further do make a just and true account of his actings and
doings therein when hereto required by the said Court and all the rest and residue of
the said Goods Chattels and Credits which shall be found remaining upon the said
Admrs. account the same being first examined

p.   Fairfax County Will Book 17th March 1746/7
197   and allowed by the Justices of the said Court for the time being shall deliver
            and pay unto such person or persons respectively as the said Justices by their
order or judgment shall direct pursuant to the Law in that Case made and provided,
And if it shall hereafter appear that any last Will and Testament was made by the said
deceased and the Executor or Exrs. therein named do exhibit the same unto the said
Court making request to have it allowed and approved accordingly the said WILLIAM
being thereunto required to render and deliver up his Letters of Administration
approbation of such Testament being first had and made in the said Court then the
Obligation to be void else to remain in full force and vertue.
            Sealed and Delivered in presence of   WILLIAM JANNEY [seal]
                                                       JOHN EVANS [seal]
At a Court held for Fairfax County March the 17th 1746.
WILLIAM JANNEY & JOHN EVANS acknowledged this Bond to be their Act and Deed
which is admitted to record.   Test   CATESBY COCKE, Cl. Cur.

-Know all men by these presents that we WILLIAM PAYNE & JOHN MINOR are held and firmly bound unto JOHN COLVILL, Gent. first Justice in the Commission of the peace for Fairfax County for and in behalf and to the sole use and behoof of the Justices of the said County and their Successors in the sum of one hundred pounds sterling to be paid to the said JOHN COLVILL his Executors Admrs. and assigns to the which payment well and truly to be made we bind ourselves and every of us our and every of our heirs Executors and Admrs. jointly and severally firmly by these presents sealed with our seals dated this 17th day of March 1746.

The Condition of this Obligation is such that if the above bound WILLIAM PAYNE Admr. of all the Goods Chattels and Credits of BENJAMIN RICHARDS deceased do make or cause to be made a true and perfect Inventory of all and singular the Goods Chattels and Credits of the said deceased which have or shall come to the hands possession or knowledge of the said WILLIAM do unto the hands or possession of any other person or persons for him, and the same so made do exhibit or cause to be exhibited into the County Court of Fairfax at such time as he shall be thereto required by the said Court and the same Goods Chattels and Credits and all other the Goods Chattels and Credits of the said deceased at the time of his death or which at any time shall come to the hands or possession of the said WILLIAM or unto the hands or possession of any other person or persons for him do well and truly administer according to law and further do make a just and true account of his actings and doings therein when

p.   Fairfax County Will Book 17th March 1746/7

198   hereto required by the said Court and all the rest and residue of and

and allowed by the Justices of the said Court for the time being shall deliver and pay unto such person or persons respectively as the said Justices by their order or judgment shall direct pursuant to the Law in that Case made and provided, And if it shall hereafter appear that any last Will and Testament was made by the said deceased and the Executor or Exrs. therein named do exhibit the same unto the said Court making request to have it allowed and approved accordingly the said WILLIAM being thereunto required to render and deliver up his Letters of Administration approbation of such Testament being first had and made in the said Court Then the Obligation to be void else to remain in full force and vertue.

Sealed and Delivered in presence of   WILLIAM PAYNE [seal]

JOHN MINOR [seal]

At a Court held for Fairfax County March the 17th 1746.

WILLIAM PAYNE & JOHN MINOR acknowledged this Bond to be their Act and Deed which is admitted to record.   Test   CATESBY COCKE, Cl. Cur.

-Know all men by these presents that we WILLIAM BRUMMEL and GARRARD TRAMEL are held and firmly bound unto JOHN COLVILL, Gent. first Justice in the Commission of the peace for Fairfax County for and in behalf and to the sole use and behoof of the Justices of the said County and their Successors in the sum of one hundred pounds sterling to be paid to the said JOHN COLVILL his Executors Admrs. and assigns to the which payment well and truly to be made we bind ourselves and every of us our and every of our heirs Executors and Admrs. jointly and severally firmly by these presents sealed with our seals dated this 17th day of March 1746.

The Condition of this Obligation is such that if the above bound WILLIAM BRUMMEL Admr. of all the Goods Chattels and Credits of JODIE BRUNO deceased do make or cause to be made a true and perfect Inventory of all and singular the Goods Chattels and Credits of the said deceased which have or shall come to the hands possession or knowledge of the said WILLIAM do unto the hands or possession of any other person or persons for him, and the same so made do exhibit or cause to be exhibited into the County Court of Fairfax at such time as he shall be thereto required by the said Court and the same Goods Chattels and Credits and all other the Goods Chattels and Credits of the said deceased at the time of his death or which at any time shall come to the hands or possession of the said WILLIAM or unto the hands or possession of any other person or persons for him and the same so made

p.   Fairfax County Will Book 17th March 1746/7
199   do exhibit or cause to be exhibited into the County Court of Fairfax at such time as he shall be thereto required by the said Court and the same Goods Chattels and Credits and all other the Goods Chattels and Credits of the said deceased at the time of his death or which at any time shall come to the hands or possession of the said WILLIAM or unto the hands or possession of any other person or persons for him do well and truly administer according to law and further do make a just and true account of his actings and doings therein when hereto required by the said Court and all the rest and residue of and allowed by the Justices of the said Court for the time being shall deliver and pay unto such person or persons respectively as the said Justices by their order or judgment shall direct pursuant to the Law in that Case made and provided, And if it shall hereafter appear that any last Will and Testament was made by the said deceased and the Executor or Exrs. therein named do exhibit the same unto the said Court making request to have it allowed and approved accordingly the said WILLIAM being thereunto required to render and deliver up his Letters of Administration approbation of such Testament being first had and made in the said Court Then the Obligation to be void else to remain in full force and vertue.

Sealed and Delivered in presence of   WILLIAM W [his mark] BRUMMEL [seal]
                                        GARRARD IT [his mark] TRAMEL [seal]
                                        DANIEL T [his mark] TRAMEL [seal]
At a Court held for Fairfax County March the 17th 1746.
WILLIAM BRUMMEL, GARRARD TRAMEL & DANIEL TRAMEL acknowledged this Bond to be their Act and Deed which is admitted to record.
            Test   CATESBY COCKE, Cl. Cur.

-March 17th 1746/7 An Inventory of the estate of LYDIA NEALE deceased

To one horse	8.0.0
To one young mare	0.15.0
To one old side saddle	0.10.0
To a parcel of coppers tools	0.6.0
To half a dozen tea spoons and tong	1.15.0
To one pair silver buttons	0.2.6
To two old gold rings	0.10.0
To one old pair silver shoe buckles	0.5.0

To one old pail and two piggins	0.5.0
To one coffee pot	0.2.6
To four tin pans and one tin bucket	0.3.0
To one box iron	0.4.0

p.
200

Fairfax County Will Book 17th March 1746/7

To her wearing cloths	4.4.0
To some bed cloths	0.10.0
To some old tea ware	0.2.6
To some coffey	0.1.0
To one tin culener	0.2.0
To one bottle snuff	0.2.0
To some flax seed	0.1.0
To one old spinning wheel	0.5.0
To one old hackel	0.2.6
To one pair cotton cards	0.3.0
To one old last hat and old knife box	0.3.0
Bedstead	0.5.0
To a corn barrel	0.2.0
JAMES DONALDSON	£19.7.6
WILLIAM SHORTRIDGE	
THOMAS WREN	

At a Court held for Fairfax County March 17th 1746.
This Inventory and appraisement of the Estate of LYDIA NEALE deceased was
returned and admitted to record.   Test   CATESBY COCKE, Cl. Cur.

-Fairfax Court Novemer the 9th 1745. In Obedience to the Worshipful Court.
We the Appraisers of the Estate of CHARLES ONEAL deceased Vizt.

To 1 fiddle	0.10.0	To 1 fron & pr. gloves & some thread	0.4.6
To 1 Jacket	0.6.0	To 1 pair old shoes	0.0.6
To 1 shirt	0.4.0	To 32 sheets of paper	0.2.0
To 1 pair leather breeches	0.4.0	To 1 handchief 1 file & chissel	0.2.4
To 1 silk cap	0.2.6		£2.7.10
To 1 ax	0.4.0	JOHN GLADDEN	
To 1 razor	0.1.6	JOHN HARTLEY	
To 1 hat	0.5.6	THOMAS WHITFORD	
To 1 gun barrel and lock	0.5.0		

At a Court continued and held for Fairfax County July the 21st 1747.
This Inventory and appraisement of the Estate of CHARLES ONEALE being returned is
admitted to record.   Test   JOHN GRAHAM, Cl. Cur.

p.
201

Fairfax County Will Book 21st July 1747

-1746 Dr. The Estate of SIMON PEARSON to WILLIAM HENRY TERRELL

	# Tob		
To 1 felt hat	10	Brought up	4408 3/4
To 3 yards brown linnen	20	To 1 pair leather	
To 2 pair stockings	30	breeches	80

To 2 ¼ yards brown holland 90
To 1 ¼ yrds tustian & jacket 42 ½
To 2/3 of Clerks Fees and Elsey 18 ¾
To 2/3 of the Quit Rents 536
To paid Mr. BROADWATER ½ a
    years board 500
To paid 1 ditto for your part of
    shoes per JOE & TOM 67
To paid ditto per stockings and ditto 33
To paid ditto per a pair stockings
    and yourself 30
To paid ditto per a 2 pair shoes
    per yourself 50
To paid ditto for making jacket
and breeches for JOE ditto for TOM 40
To paid ditto for making 2 shifts
and let and negro childrens cloaths 20
To paid ditto your part of 700 8#
nails for rolling crop 1744 20
To paid ditto for making you 6 shirts 45
To paid ditto your part for
    laying an ax 13
To paid ditto your part of SMITH
    paid FRANCIS TRIPLET 65
To paid ditto your part of JOE's Levy 22 1/2
To 1 ¾ yrds check 1 ½ yds brown
    Holland 75
To 1 yard black ribbon 1 pair
    Buckles 33 1/2
To 1 fine hat 1 felt ditto making
    1 shirt 82 1/2
To 12 yds best cotton 8 yrds
    course ditto 396
To ¾# bro thread 20 yrds bro
    Linnen 193 1/2
To one years board 1000
To paid DAVIS & HEYSEN
    per schooling 418
To 7 seams blen thread 4
To 2 yards red callimanco 36
To 1 yrd red shaloon 2 yds
    blen famy 45
To 2 doz. mohair buttn. 3 stks hair 25
To 1 doz. vest buttons 6 ¼
    yrds drugget 135
To 1 ½ yds fine bro linned 1 yrd
    course ditto 19

to 1 pair fine yard stockins
    pr course ditto 70
To making 2 shirts 15
To paid DAVID THOMAS per
making a coat & 2 jackets 80
To 1 pair shoes 30
To 3 ¾ yrds. Brown holland 150
To 10 seams thread &
    1 stick hair 5
To 1 pair of knee and shoe
    buckles 17
To 1 yard callimanco <u>18</u>
    # Tob. 5801 3/4
E Excepted per
    WILLIAM HENRY TERRELL
At a Court held for Fairfax County
the 21st day of July 1747.
WILLIAM HENRY TERRELL
Guardian to SIMON PEARSON
exhibited this account and made
oath thereto which is allowed of by
the Court and admitted to record.
Test · JOHN GRAHAM, Cl. Cur.

```
To 2/3 of 2500 10# nails
        to hunt                        126 1/2
To paid ROBERT FOSTER for
        taking up His mare             50
To 3 ½ yds check 1 pair shoes          84
                                       4408
```

p. <u>Fairfax County Will Book 21st July 1747</u>
202 -Pursuant to an order of Fairfax County Court dated the 17th September 1746.
    We the Subscribers being first sworn before Capt. JOHN WEST did meet and
appraise the Estate of JOHN MUSGROVE deceased Vizt.

```
To 1 corner cuberd & tea table         0.15.0
To 1 sow and piggs and 3 shoats        0.16.0
To 15 head of hogs at 8/ per peace     6
To 7 small shoats                      3
            SAMPSON DARRELL            7.14
            WILLIAM x [his mark] MOXLEY
            SAMUEL MOXLEY
```

At a Court held for Fairfax County the 21st day of July 1747.
This Inventory and appraisement of the Estate of JOHN MUSGROVE deceased being
admitted to record.   Test   JOHN GRAHAM, Cl. Cur.

-An Inventory of the Estate of WILLIAM GRIMWOOD deceased appraised April
the 11th 1747.

```
To 12 pewter plates 6 candles 5s                                    0.17.0
To 12 pewter tankard                                                0.2.0
To 4 pewter dishes                                                  0.16.0
To 3 pewter basons                                                  0.6.0
To 29 pieces small delft ware at 2d per                             0.4.6
To 11 pieces glassware at 4d per                                    0.3.8
To 20 Tin canasters at 6d 1 tin sugar box 2/                        0.3.8
To 1 tin cullinder 2/ 1 tin dripping pan 2/ 4 tin dish cover 2s     0.6.0
To 1 tin candle box 8d 1 tin lamp 8d 1 tin candlestick 8d           0.2.0
To 1 horass sickle 11 morter and pestle 1 cooper tea kettle         1.10.0
        To 1 copper coffee pot 1 brass sten pot cover and hocks
To ½ dozen table knives and fortes                                  0.2.0
To 6 glass bottles                                                  0.1.6
To 1 iron pot and hoods 5/6d 2 iron candlesticks at 6d per          0.6.6
To 1 grid iron 2/ 1 doz/ scences & hooks 2/6d                       0.5.6
        1 pr. cacket stillards 1/
To 2 brass pepper boxes 18d 1 box iron & 2 heaters 18d              0.3.0
To 1 shovel and 1 pr. tongs 3/ 1 frying pan and ladle 18d           0.5.0
To 1 chafing dish and bird roaster hooks                            0.1.6
To 1 gun 20s 1 hanger and belt 4/6                                  1.4.6
To 1 pair bellows 8d 6 Glagg bottomd chairs at 1/6                  0.6.8
To 1 trundle bed stead cord & hyde feather bed bolster              4.10.0
        & 2 pillows 2 sheets 1 rugg & 1 pr. blankets (1 old sheet)
```

To 1 desk 15/ 1 table 10/	1.5.0
To 1 clo brush 1 tin grater 1 looking glass 1 peagon	0.3.0
To 1 grey horse and saddle	3.0.0
To 1 set iron wedges 8/2 2 narrow axes 1/ 1 auger & spike gimblet 1/	0.8.0
To 1 saw 1/ 1 drawing knife 1/ 4 old hoes 3/6	0.5.6
To 2 boxes 2/6d 3 old tubbs 18d 1 bed stead cord & 2 old Tick 2/6d	0.6.6
To a set of barbers tools	2.0.0

p. 203 <u>Fairfax County Will Book 21st July 1747</u>

To hairs of all kinds	3.0.0
To 2 wiggs & 1 grindstone 12/6 1 pair & orange strainer & 1 mustard bottle 6 tea spoons 5d	<u>0.18.6</u>
Appraised by us the date above	23.3.6

RICHARD OSBORN
DANIEL FRENCH
THOMAS LEWIS

At a Court held for Fairfax County July the 21st 1747.
This Inventory and appraisement of the Estate of WILLIAM GRIMWOOD deceased being returned and admitted to record.   Test   JOHN GRAHAM, Cl. Cur.

-The Inventory of the Goods belonging to the Estate of MARK THOMAS deceased that is laid before us appointed to appraise the same April the 3rd 1747.
JOSEPH McGEACH, JOSEPH WEST, FRANCIS WILKS

To 1 old saddle	0.1.0
To 1 pine chest with lock and shey	0.5.0
To 1 white wigg and pair of old books	0.1.0
To 1 pair of new shoes	0.6.0
To 1 felt and old custom hats	0.1.6
To 2 pair old breeches 1 pair draws	0.1.6
To 1 coat and jacket	0.7.6
To 5 shirts and 2 pair stockings	0.14.0
To 3 handc and 1 cap	0.3.2
To 1 pair old shoes 2 pair thread stocking and garters	0.5.2
To a remnant of ornabrign	0.1.0
To powder and lead and a bottle	0.4.4
To 4 bottles 1 old canester with mustard seed	0.1.6
To 1 white handc. with sundry of old buckles buttons fish hooks And curtin hinges	0.1.6
To 3 spoons 2 knives 1 pair sisars 1 pair fleams 2 tobacco boxes 1 brush 1 goard with sugar 1 goard with gun flints 1 belt	0.4.7
To books and raggs	0.3.0
To 1 old chest and padlock	0.2.6
To 1 whitish coloured bule	1.0.0
To money scales and weights	0.5.0
To 1 old gun and shot bag and horn	0.10.0

To 1 old bed and bolster		0.10.0	
To 1 heifer 18 months old		0.18.0	
To 1 burning iron		<u>0.0.4</u>	

At a Court held for Fairfax County July the 21st 1747.　　　　£6.7.7

This Inventory and appraisement of the Estate of MARK THOMAS deceased was returned and admitted to record.　　Test　　JOHN GRAHAM, Cl. Cur.

p.　　<u>Fairfax County Will Book 21st July 1747</u>

204　　-May 18 1747　　　　We the subscribers being first sworn have Inventoryed & appraised all and singular the Estate of JOHN BRUMMEL deceased that was presented to our View Vizt.

To 1 gun barrel & lock	0.10.0	To 1 bed and furniture	4.0.0
To 1 old saddle	0.2.6	To 1 old chest	0.2.6
To 1 side of leather	0.6.0	To 17 hoggs at 6s	5.2.0
To 2 pair of old shoes		To 15 piggs	0.15.0
1 pair of old boots	0.8.0	To cash	3.16.1
To 1 pair of claps	0.2.6	To 1 mare and colt	<u>2.15.0</u>
To a parcel of old clove	0.15.0		£37.12.8
To a parcel of new clove	2.15.0		
To new & old wearing linnen	1.15.0	JOHN ASHFORD	
To 1 saddle & two housens	2.0.0	WILLIAM x [his mark] TRAMMEL	
To 2 horses	8.0.0	EDWARD VILET	
To 1 cow and yearlin	2.0.0		
To 10 barrels of corn at 4s	2.0.0		
To 1 sord at 5/1 hand	0.6.0		
To a parcel of old iron	0.1.8		

At a Court held for Fairfax County July the 21st 1747.

This Inventory and appraisement of the Estate of JOHN BRUMMEL deceased was returned and admitted to record.　　Test　　JOHN GRAHAM, Cl. Cur.

-Dr.　　The Estate of BENJAMIN HALLING deceased

To paid JOHN GILESSON		1250	By the whole amount of the
To paid JOSEPH WILSON	0.15.0		Estate as per appraisement
To paid WILLIAM HALLING	4.1.9		in the office will appear
To paid MARY McDOWELL		800	
To paid LAWRENCE YANCHAM	0.17.0		33.0.0
To paid PRECELLA WILSON	0.14.11		At a Court continued and
To paid JOSEPH WILSON	1.2.7 ½		held for Fairfax County the
To paid ditto	0.17.9		22nd of July 1747.
To paid HUGH WEST	1.4.4		
To paid JOHN EVANS		1050	ANN HALLING Admrx. of
To 6 percent for collecting paying	1.3.7	186	BENJAMIN HALLING
And charges of Adrmrs.			Deceased exhibited this
			Account against the

Descendants Estate and made oath thereto which was allowed and admitted to record.　　　　Test　　JOHN GRAHAM, Cl. Cur.

-Know all men by these presents that we JANE SCANLIN, HENRY JENNINGS and JAMES MURREY are held and firmly bound unto JOHN COLVILL, Gent. first Justice in Commission of the peace for Fairfax County for and in behalf and to the sole use and behoof of the Justices of the said County and their Successors in the sum of two hundred pounds sterling to be paid to the said JOHN COLVILL his Executors Administrators and assigns t the which payment well and truly made we bind ourselves and every of us our and every of our heirs Executors and

p.   Fairfax County Will Book 21st July 1747
205   Administrators jointly and severally firmly by these presents scaled with our seales dated this 21st day of July 1747. The Condition of this Obligation is such that if the above bound JANE SCANLIN Admrx. of all the Goods Chattels and Credits of THOMAS SCANLIN deceased do make or cause to be made a true and perfect Inventory of all and singular the Goods Chattels and Credits of the said deceased which have or shall come to the hands possession or knowledge of the said JANE or unto the hands or possession of any other person or persons for her and the same so made do exhibit or cause to be exhibited into the County Court of Fairfax at such time as she shall be thereto required by the Court and the same Goods Chattels and Credits and all other the Goods Chattels and Credits of the said Deceased at the time of his Death or which at any time after shall come to the hands or possession of the said JANE or into the hands or possession of any other person or persons do well and truly administer according to Law and further do make a just and true account of her actings and doings therein when thereunto required by the said Court and all the rest and residue of the said Goods Chattels and Credits which shall be found upon the said Admrx. account the same being first examined and allowed by the Justices of the said Court for the time being shall deliver and pay unto such person or persons respectively as the said Justices by their order or Judgment shall direct pursuant to the Law in that case made and provided and if it shall hereafter appear that any last Will and Testament was made by the said deceased and the Executor or executors therein named do exhibit the same into the said Court making request to have it allowed and approved accordingly if the said JANE being thereunto required do render and deliver up Letters of Administration approbation of such Testament being first had and made in the said Court then this obligation to be void else to remain in full force and virtue.

Sealed and delivered in presents of   JANE X [her mark] SCANLIN [seal]
                                             HENRY H [his mark] JENNINGS [seal]
                                             JAMES X [his mark] MURREY [seal]
At a Court held for Fairfax County this 21st day of July 1747.
JANE SCANLIN, HENRY JENNINGS and JAMES MURREY acknowledged this Bond to be their Act and Deed and is admitted to record. Test   JOHN GRAHAM, Cl. Cur.

-Know all men by these presents that We JOHN CARLYLE, JOHN PAGAN, GARRARD ALEXANDER & HARRY PIPER are held and firmly bound unto JOHN COLVILL, Gent. first Justice in Commission of the peace for Fairfax County for and in behalf and to the sole use and behoof of the Justices of the said County and their Successors in the sum of one thousand pounds sterling to be paid to the said JOHN COLVILL his Executors Administrators and assigns the which payment well and truly made we bind ourselves and every of us our and every of our heirs Executors and Administrators jointly and severally firmly by these presents sealed with our seales dated this xxii day of July 1747. The Condition of this Obligation is such that if the above bound JOHN CARLYLE and JOHN PAGAN Admrs. of all the Goods Chattels and Credits of RICHARD POULTNEY deceased do make or cause to be made a true and perfect Inventory of all and singular the Goods Chattels and Credits of the said deceased which have or shall come to the hands possession or knowledge of the said CARLYLE and PAGAN or unto the

p.　　Fairfax County Will Book 23rd July 1747

206　　hands or possession of any other person or persons for them and the same so made do exhibit or cause to be exhibited into the County Court of Fairfax at such time as they shall be thereto required by the Court and the same Goods Chattels and Credits and all other the Goods Chattels and Credits of the said Deceased at the time of his Death or which at any time after shall come to the hands or possession of the said CARLYLE and PAGAN or into the hands or possession of any other person or persons do well and truly administer according to Law and further do make a just and true account of their actings and doings therein when thereto required by the said Court and all the rest and residue of the said Goods Chattels and Credits which shall be found upon the said Admrs. account the same being first examined and allowed by the Justices of the said Court for the time being shall deliver and pay unto such person or persons respectively as the said Justices by their order or Judgment shall direct pursuant to the Law in that case made and provided and if it shall hereafter appear that any last Will and Testament was made by the said deceased and the Executor or Executors therein named do exhibit the same into the said Court making request to have it allowed and approved accordingly if the said Admrs. being thereunto required do render and deliver up their Letters of Administration approbation of such Testament being first had and made in the said Court then this obligation to be void else to remain in full force and virtue.

Sealed and delivered in presence of　　JOHN CARLYLE [seal]
　　　　　　　　　　　　　　　　　　　JOHN PAGAN [seal]
　　　　　　　　　　　　　　　　　　　GARRARD ALEXANDER [seal]
　　　　　　　　　　　　　　　　　　　HARRY PIPER [seal]

At a Court held for Fairfax County the 23rd of July 1747.
JOHN CARLYLE, JOHN PAGAN, GARRARD ALEXANDER and HARRY PIPER acknowledged this Bond to be their Acts and Deeds and admitted to record.
　　　　　　Test　　JOHN GRAHAM, Cl. Cur.

-The Estate of WILLIAM GRIMWOOD, deceased Dr	Contra
To funeral expenses	1.8.0
To 2 gallons rum at the sale and appraisment 12s	0.12.0
To auctioner of Settling the several accts. 20s	1.6.0
To 3 appraisers fees	0.9.0
To paid Capt. OSBORN for the sheriff 247	12.11.11
To paid Maj. WASHINGTON as per account	7.16.3 1/2
To paid JOHN GLADING as per account proved	3.9.10 1/2
To paid JOHN CARLYLE as per account proved	5.10.0

To Clerks fees and Secretarys fees

[Contra] By the amount of the Estate after sale   £23.4.0

At a Court held for Fairfax County the 18th of August 1747.

JOHN NORTH exhibited this account against the Estate of WILLIAM GRIMWOOD and made oath thereto which is allowed of and admitted to record.

Test   JOHN GRAHAM, Cl. Cur.

-Know all men by these presents that We MARY JANNEY, FRANCIS HAGUE, JOHN HOUGH, BENJAMIN SEBASTIAN & THOMAS WREN are held and firmly bound unto JOHN COLVILL, Gent. first Justice in Commission of the peace for Fairfax County for and in behalf and to the sole use and behoof of the Justices of the said County and their Successors in the sum of one thousand pounds sterling to be paid to the said JOHN COLVILL his Executors Administrators and assigns to which

p.   Fairfax County Will Book 18th August 1747

207   payment well and truly made we bind ourselves and every of us our and every of our heirs Executors and Administrators jointly and severally firmly by these presents sealed with our seales dated this 18th day of August 1747. The Condition of this Obligation is such that if the above bound MARY JANNEY & FRANCIS HAGUE Admrs. of all the Goods Chattels and Credits of AMOS JANNEY deceased do make or cause to be made a true and perfect Inventory of all and singular the Goods Chattels and Credits of the said deceased which have or shall come to the hands possession or knowledge of the said MARY & FRANCIS or unto the hands or possession of any other person or persons for them and the same so made do exhibit or cause to be exhibited into the County Court of Fairfax at such time as they shall be thereto required by the Court and the same Goods Chattels and Credits and all other the Goods Chattels and Credits of the said Deceased at the time of his Death or which at any time after shall come to the hands or possession of the said MARY and FRANCIS or into the hands or possession of any other person or persons do well and truly administer according to Law and further do make a just and true account of their actings and doings therein when thereto required by the said Court and all the rest and residue of the said Goods Chattels and Credits which shall be found upon the said Adrnrs. account the same being first examined and allowed by the Justices of the said Court for the time being shall deliver and pay unto such person or persons respectively as the said Justices by their order or Judgment shall direct pursuant to the Law in that case made and provided and if it shall hereafter appear that any last Will and Testament was made by the said deceased and the Executor or Executors therein named do exhibit the same into the said Court making request to have it allowed and approved accordingly if the said Admrs. being thereunto required do render and deliver up their Letters of Administration approbation of such Testament being first had and made in the said Court then this obligation to be void else to remain in full force and virtue.

Sealed and delivered in presence of

MARY JANNEY [seal]
FRANCIS HAGUE [seal]
JOHN HOUGH [seal]
BENJAMIN SEBASTIAN [seal]
THOMAS WREN [seal]

At a Court held for Fairfax County the 18th day of August 1747.
MARY JANNEY, FRANCIS HAGUE, JOHN HOUGH, BENJAMIN SEBASTIAN & THOMAS
WREN acknowledge this Bond to be their Acts and Deeds and admitted to record.
Test   JOHN GRAHAM, Cl. Cur.

-A true and perfect Inventory of the Estate of THOMAS SCANLIN deceased.

To one large iron bound chest	0.12.6	To three pails 6/ three piggins 4s	
To one small ditto	0.4.0	and a washing tub	0.11.6
To one box 2/6 two old broken		To two wooden chairs 6/ two old	
Boxes and a lock and key 1/ one		ditto 2/6	0.7.6
Powder horn & shot bag	0.3.3	To a parcel of cooper tools 8/2	
To one old tub gum and sifter	0.2.0	knives & forks	0.9.0
To five tubbs 2 gums and old		To a parcel of carpenters tools 8/6	
Bucket and a rundlet 7/ a hogshead		one frying pan 4/	0.12.6
& 2 cash 8/	0.12.0	To a parcel of shoemakers tools	0.4.6
To a parcel of wooden ware	0.5.0	To half a dozen reap hooks	0.3.0

p.   Fairfax County Will Book 19th August 1747

208 To two tin pans one sauce pan		To one horse	3.0.0
one canister one sugar box one		To one young ditto	1.15.0
one old funnel	0.6.0	To eleven sows & barrow's at 6/	3.6.0
To three earthen mugs stop bason		To twenty three pigs at 1/	1.3.0
And candlestick	0.1.8	To one rugg	0.7.0
To one hominey sifter bell & wool		To one feather bed and bolster rug	
Cards	0.1.0	blankets sheets standing bed sted	
To 1 sifter and salt box	0.0.9	cord and hide	5.0.0
To three old razor blades & two		To one trundle bed sted & ditto	4.0.0
Old buckles	0.0.6	To one feather bed & bolster rug	
To a bell and coller	0.3.6	blankets standing bed sted cord	
To one saddle and bridle	0.15.0	and hide	3.0.0
To one box iron and heaters	0.7.6	To an old rug bed tick pillow spur	
To 1 grindstone	0.3.0	and piece of curried leather	0.1.6
To 1 pestle flesh forks & piece of		To one dish bason and plate	0.8.0
Of old iron	0.5.6	To three pewter dishes six plates	
To one pr. sheep shears &		one porringes three basons &	
Candlestick	0.1.3	eighteen spoons	1.8.6
To one plough & 4 old stove	0.4.0	To one old bason dish two plates	
To 2 axes	0.5.0	tankard and eight spoons	0.8.6
To a set of wedges	0.4.0	To one iron pot and hooks	0.7.5
To a cross cut saw	0.7.6	To one kettle cracked	0.3.6
To fourteen pounds of old iron	0.2.0	To one iron skillet	0.2.6
To a sword & cutooch iron	0.12.0	To one coat 2 jackets & 2 pr	
To ½ a dozen bottles	0.1.0	breeches	0.10.0
To eight pounds spun cotton	0.16.0	To one hat 5/ two baggs & a	
To one large oval table	2.5.0	wallet 4/	0.9.0
To one small table and form	0.3.0	To two old shirts	0.3.0
To one spinning wheel	0.3.0	To one pr. hose	0.2.6

To one deer skin	0.4.0			44.7.6
To one cows hyde	0.4.0	JANE I [her mark] SCANLIN, Admrx.		15.6.7
To eight sows and barrows	2.8.0	Fairfax County		£59.14.1
To one small jugg	0.1.6	In Obedience to an order of Court dated the 21st
To 1 pair of sheers	0.0.8	July 1747. We the Subscribers under mentioned
	15.6.7	being appointed by the said Court to value the
To one servant man having	1.0.0	Estate of THOMAS SCANLIN deceased and being
11 Months to serve		first sworn We did value and appraise all the said
To one cow and calf	2.0.0	SCANLIN's Estate as was presented to our view
To one heifer and calf	1.15.0	as is set forth in this Inventory. Witness our
To 3 cows at 38/	5.14.0	hands this day of	JOHN GIST
To one large steer	2.5.0		JOHN PEAKE, Junior
To one small ditto	0.18.0		JOHN NORWOOD
To two heifers at 15/	1.10.0	At a Court continued and held for Fairfax County
To two ditto at 10/	1.0.0	the 19th day of August 1747.
To one cow	1.5.0	This Inventory and appraisement of the Estate of
To one bull	1.5.0	THOMAS SCANLIN being returned is admitted to
		To record. Test JOHN GRAHAM, Cl. Cur.

p.   Fairfax County Will Book 15th September 1747

209   -In Obedience to an order of Court made the 18th day of March 1746 to We the Subscribers have praised all the estate that was shone to us of BENJAMIN RICHARDS according to Law as followeth.

To one cow and yearling	1.5.0
To one very old horse and very pore	0.8.0
To one old rugg 5 to 2 old boxes and saw	0.7.6
To 1 hammer and file	0.1.6
To a parcel of old iron	0.0.6
To 1 box iron and heater	0.4.0
To 2 watch and tobacco box	5.0.0
To one raisor	0.0.6

THOMAS FALKNER   7.7.0
JOHN IS [his mark] SUMMERS
WILLIAM TORBUT

At a Court held for Fairfax County September the 15 1747.

This Inventory and appraisement of the Estate of BENJAMIN RICHARDS deceased being returned is admitted to record.   Test   JOHN GRAHAM, Cl. Cur.

-1747 Mr. BENJAMIN RICHARDS deced.		Dr.	per Contra	
1743 To 1 county levy	20		By the amount of	7.7.0
1744 To one county and publick			your Estate	
levie	36		By WILLIAM	
To a gal. and half a pint of rum		1.4.4 ½	TRAMMELL	400#
To paid Mr. TERRELL for Rent	830			
To cash paid Mr. SCOTT at Williamsburg		3.9	Errors Excepted per me	
To paid ELIZABETH SANDERS		10	WILLIAM PAYNE	
To Clerks fees	120			

To Secretarys fees   36   At a Court held for Fairfax County
To a costin shirt sheet and digging   September the 15th 1747.
A grave and half a gallon of rum   550
                                      1591.1.18.1 1/2

WILLIAM PAYNE, Gent. exhibited the above account against the Estate of BENJAMIN
RICHARDS deceased and made oath thereto which is allowed and admitted to record
and the Tobacco rated at twelve shillings and six pence per cent.
                    Test   JOHN GRAHAM, Cl. Cur.

          -Know all men by these presents that we MARY JENKINS, SAMUEL JENKINS
and HENRY GUNNELL are held and firmly bound unto JOHN COLVILL, Gent. first
Justice in Commission of the peace for Fairfax County for and in behalf and to the
sole use and behoof of the Justices of the said County and their Successors in the
sum of one thousand pounds sterling to be paid to the said JOHN COLVILL his
Executors Administrators and assigns to which payment well and truly to be made we
bind ourselves and every of us our and every of our

p.   Fairfax County Will Book 17th November 1747
210   heirs Executors and Administrators jointly and severally firmly by these
          presents sealed with our seals dated this 17th day of November 1747. The
Condition of this Obligation is such that if the above bound MARY JENKINS Executrix
of the last Will and Testament of WILLIAM JENKINS do make or cause to be made a
true and perfect Inventory of all and singular the Goods Chattels and Credits of the
said deceased which have or shall come to the hands possession or knowledge of
the said MARY or unto the hands or possession of any other person or persons for
her and the same so made do exhibit or cause to be exhibited into the County Court
of Fairfax at such time as she shall be thereto required by the Court and the same
Goods Chattels and Credits and all other the Goods Chattels and Credits of the said
Deceased at the time of his Death or which at any time after shall come to the hands
or possession of the said MARY or into the hands or possession of any other person
or persons do well and truly administer according to Law and further do make a just
and true account of her actings and doings therein when thereto required by the said
Court and also do well and truly pay and deliver all the Legacies contained and
specified in the said Testament as far as the said Goods Chattels and Credits will
thereunto extend and the Law shall charge her. Then this obligation to be void else to
remain in full force and vertue.
Sealed and delivered in the presence of   MARY B [her mark] JENKINS [seal]
                                           SAMUEL x [his mark] JENKINS [seal]
                                           HENRY GUNNELL [seal]
At a Court held for Fairfax County the 17th day of November 1747.
MARY JENKINS, SAMUEL JENKINS & HENRY GUNNELL acknowledged this Bond to be
their Acts and Deeds and admitted to record.   Test   JOHN GRAHAM, Cl. Cur.

          -In the name of God Amen. I WILLIAM JENKINS of Truro Parish and the County
of Fairfax being very sick and weak of body but of perfect sense and memory and
understanding thanks be to God for the same doth make and ordain this my last Will
and Testament in manner and form following Vizt. Item I give and bequeath my sole

to god who gave it to me and by body to the ground from whence it was taken to be buried in a decent manner according to the discretion of my Executors hereafter mentioned and Lastly I shall dispose of my worldly goods which god has bestoed upon me far beyond by desarts in manner and form following.

Item I give and bequeath unto my Dearly beloved wife MARY JENKINS her first choice of all my horses or mairs for her own proper riding creature to have and to hold the same during her natural life. Item I give and bequeath unto my son SAMUEL JENKINS his next choiest of all my horses or mairs when he shall arrive at the age of eighteen years to have and to hold the same forever. Item I give and bequeath unto my son WILLIAM JENKINS when he shall arrive at the age of eighteen his choiest of either horse or mair that shall be upon the planet or arrive from any part of my now Estate. Item I give and bequeath unto my son JOB JENKINS when he arrives at the age of eighteen years his choiest in the same manner. Item it is my Will and desire that my son SAMUEL JENKINS shall have the use of my riffles and gun until my son WILLIAM doth arrive to the age of eighteen years and then return them to him the said WILLIAM JENKINS and he to have and to hold the same as his own proper writ forever. Item I give and bequeath unto my son SAMUEL JENKINS my Steel trap and my smooth barriled gun to have and to hold the same forever. Item I give and bequeath unto my son WILLIAM JENKINS all my carpenders and coopers tools to have and to hold the same as his own property forever.

p.   Fairfax County Will Book 17th November 1747

211   Item, It is my Will and desire that when my sons or either shall arrive at the age of eighteen years of age if their is not any horses or mairs for them to take my will is that my Executors hereafter mentioned doth pay unto them or either of them the sum of five pounds current money.

Item, It is my Will and desire that my dearly beloved wife shall have the sold benefit of all and singular the remainder of my personally Estate during her natural life provided she lives single or marryes a man that doth take a good care of my children and use them well, but it she doth marry a man that doth not doe well by my children my will and desire is that my Brother EZLL. JENKINS if alive should take my children and Estate out of his hands and the same to be equally divided amongst them and they to be prosest of the same at the age of eighteen years and not before but provided my Brother EZLL. JENKINS not be alive that then my Brother JOHN and JAMES JENKINS to have my children in the same manner as my Brothr EZLL. JENKINS was. Item. It is my will and desire that all my children should be for themselves at the age of eighteen years. Item, It is my will and desire that after the death of my beloved wife provided she marry a man that doth doe ever so well by my children the forementioned Legacies be excepted and paid before mentioned. Item, it is my will and desire that my dearly beloved wife should be my whole and sole Executx. of this my Will and Testament in Witness whereof I have hearunto set my hand and affixed my seal this 31st day of July 1747.

Signed Sealed and Delivered in preasants of us

WALTER ENGLISH   WILLIAM X [his mark] JENKINS [seal]
MARY M [her mark] JENKINS
WILLIAM GUY

At a Court held for Fairfax County November the 17th 1747.

This last Will and Testament of WILLIAM JENKINS deceased was presented into Court by MARY JENKINS the Executrix therein named who made oath thereto according to Law and being proved by the oaths of WALTER ENGLISH and MARY JENKINS two of the Witnesses is admitted to record and the said Executrix performing what is usual in such cases Certificate is granted her for obtaining a probate thereof in due form.
  Test JOHN GRAHAM, Cl. Cur.

  -In the name of God Amen, I JOHN EVANS of Truro Parish and Fairfax County in Virginia Tyler being of parfect health and memory and calling to mind the uncertainty of this Transetory life do make constitute ordain and appoint this to be my last Will and Testament revoking all other Wills and Testament by me at any time heretofore made Imprimis first and principality I bequeath my Soul to Allmighty God my Creator hoping thro the merits and Intersesion of my Blessed Savior and Redemer Jesus Christ to have a full pardon and Remission of all my Sins and my body to the Earth from whence it came to be entered in a desent and Christian maner at the discresion of my Exer. Hereafter named. Item, my will and desire is that all my Just debts be fully satisfyed contented and paid an as for what other worldly Estate it hath pleased God to bless me with I do give and dispose thereof in the following manner Vizt. Item, I do give and bequeath unto my loving wife MARGRAT EVANS all and singular my Estate Real and Personal to her and her heirs after her during her widowhood and in case of change then none

p. <u>Fairfax County Will Book 17th November 1747</u>
212 But her lawful due to my son JOHN EVANS and his heirs forever to be left in the hands of JOHN SUMMERS, Senior at his Descretion to bring up my child.
In Witness whereof I have hereunto set my hand seal this 26th day of August 1746.
  Sined Sealed and Delivered in the presence of
  JAMES HAMILTON, WILLIAM AMIES, GEORGE WIGHT JOHN EVANS [seal]
At a Court held for Fairfax County the 17th day of November 1747.
The last Will and Testament of JOHN EVANS deceased was presented into Court by MARGARET EVANS who made oath thereto according to Law, and being proved by the oaths of JAMES HAMILTON, WILLIAM AMIES and GEORGE WIGHT Evidences thereto is admitted to record and the said MARGARET performing what is usual in such cases Certificate is granted her for obtaining Letters of Administration with the said Will annexed in due form. Test JOHN GRAHAM, Cl. Cur.

  -In Obedience to an order of this Court we whose names ware under writting being first sworne we have praised and valued all the Estate of JOHN HALLING deced. as came to hour view &c.

To 1 gray mair	5.0.0	To 1 old saddle	0.5.0
To 1 bay horse	5.0.0	To 12 barrows 1 boar	
To 1 old bed of turkeys ferrors and		6 sows and pigs	8.15.0
6 old blankets & bedsted	1.10.0	To 1 gunn	1.5.0
To Wedding ware	0.1.8	To 1 colt	1.10.0
To 11 duft tales inges	0.6.0	To 1 young bull	0.16.8
To 1 frier pan 1 plain & ink holder	0.6.0	To 4 tin pans	0.8.0
To 1 hand saw 6/ to old clase 2/6d	0.8.0		£25.11.10

May 15th 1747
Appraisers   THOMAS AWBREY, PHILIP NOLAND, JOHN GORDON
At a Court held for Fairfax County the 17th day of November 1747.
This Inventory and appraisment of the Estate of JOHN HALLING deceased was
returned and admitted to record.   Test   JOHN GRAHAM, Cl. Cur.

-The Remainder of the Estate of AGNES BRONAUGH which was not aprased by
the said men apinted by the worshipful Court by reson I cold not bring them to view
but sence I have brought them to view &c the aprasers valeth them in money as
apereth.   To 3 hoggs at   1.5.0
                    To some old iron at   0.5.0
          WILLIAM BRONAUGH   1.10.0
At a Court continued and held for Fairfax County November the 19th 1747.
This additional Inventory and appraisement of the Estate of AGNES BRONAUGH
deceased was returned and admitted to record.   Test   JOHN GRAHAM, Cl. Cur.

p.   Fairfax County Will Book 17th November 1747
213   1742 Dr.   The Estate of Mr. ROBERT OSBORN deceased
          7.17 1745 To accot. settled with Fairfax Court   13498
To Ball. Given Cr. For in Cash 12/6 per   885
                                                                            14388
To Cash accot. Settled with the Court per vouchers &c   50.18.2 ½
To MARTIN FRANCIS per acct. Proved   0.16.0
To JOHN GLADING per ditto   0.4.0
To Mr. HENRY WATSON   1.14.3
To 1129# Tob. to JOHN BALL at 12/6 percent   7.1.1 ½
                                                                            £60.13.4
To Ballance of the Credit side   41.11.7
To 1 Negro Boy sold Mr. JOHN CARLYLE   25.0.0
                                                                            66.11.7
To Ballance due to the Estate clear   135.16.4
                                                                            £212.7.11
Cr.   7.17 1745 By accot. Settled   14388
          By cash acct settled with the Court   6.15.0
          By 885# Tobacco of the Dr. side to Ballc.   5.10.7 ½
              Tobacco acct at 12/6
          By 846# Tob. per Mrs. ANN OSBORN at ditto   5.5.9
          By overcharged the Estate 1.0.3 sterl to   1.10.4 1/2
            Mr. HENRY THRELKELD 50 percent thereon   19.1.9
          By ballance due to RICHARD OSBORN, Ex.   41.11.7
          By ditto for copy Inventory & account   £60.13.4
            & according accts. In Tobacco   #tob 40
          By Inventory of the whole Estate   £202.7.11
                    RICHARD OSBORN Executor
At a Court continued and held for Fairfax County November the 18th 1747.

RICHARD OSBORN, Gent. exhibited the above account against the Estate of ROBERT OSBORN deceased and made oath thereto which is allowed of and admitted to record.   Test   JOHN GRAHAM, Cl. Cur.

        -Know all men by these presents that we MARGARET EVANS, THOMAS WREN and THOMAS FALKNER are held and firmly bound unto JOHN COLVILL, Gent. first Justice in Commission of the peace for Fairfax County for and in behalf and to the sole use and behoof of the Justices of the said County and their Successors in the sum of three hundred pounds sterling to be paid to the said JOHN COLVILL his Executors Administrators and assigns to which payment well and truly to be made we bind ourselves and every of us our and every of our heirs Executors and Administrators jointly and severally firmly by these presents sealed with our seals dated this 17th day of November 1747. The Condition of this Obligation is such that if the above bound MARGARET EVANS Admrx. of the last Will and Testament of JOHN EVANS deceased thereunto annexed do make or cause to be made a true and perfect Inventory of all and singular the Goods Chattels and Credits of the said deceased which have or shall come to the hands possession or knowledge of the said MARGARET or unto the hands or possession of any other person or persons for her and the same so made do exhibit or cause to be exhibited into the County Court of Fairfax at such time as she shall be thereto required by the Court and the same Goods Chattels and Credits and all other the Goods Chattels and Credits of the said Deceased at the time of his Death or which at any time after shall come to the hands or possession of the said MARGARET or into the hands or possession of any other person or persons do well and truly administer according to Law and further do make a just and true account of her actings and doings therein when thereto required by the said Court and also do well and truly pay and deliver all the Legacies contained and specified in the said Testament as far as the said Goods Chattels and Credits will thereunto extend and the Law shall charge her. Then this obligation to be void else to remain in full force and vertue.
Sealed and delivered in the presence of   MARGARET W [her mark] EVANS [seal]
                                            THOMAS WREN [seal]
                                            THOMAS FALKNER [seal]

p.   Fairfax County Will Book 18th November 1747
214   At a Court held for Fairfax County November the 17th 1747.
        MARGARET EVANS, THOMAS WREN and THOMAS FALKNER acknowledged the aforegoing Bond to be their Acts and Deeds and is admitted to record.
                Test   JOHN GRAHAM, Cl. Cur.
        -Know all men by these presents that we WILLIAM SENT, GARRARD TRAMMELL and WALTER ENGLISH are held and firmly bound unto JOHN COLVILL, Gent. first Justice in Commission of the peace for Fairfax County for and in behalf and to the sole use and behoof of the Justices of the said County and their Successors in the sum of two hundred pounds sterling to be paid to the said JOHN COLVILL his Executors Administrators and assigns to which payment well and truly to be made we bind ourselves and every of us our and every of our heirs Executors and Administrators jointly and severally firmly by these presents sealed with our seals dated this 18th day of November 1747. The Condition of this Obligation is such that

if the above bound WILLIAM SENT Admr. of the last Will and Testament of DAVID JONES deceased thereunto annexed do make or cause to be made a true and perfect Inventory of all and singular the Goods Chattels and Credits of the said deceased which have or shall come to the hands possession or knowledge of the said WILLIAM or unto the hands or possession of any other person or persons for him and the same so made do exhibit or cause to be exhibited into the County Court of Fairfax at such time as he shall be thereto required by the Court and the same Goods Chattels and Credits and all other the Goods Chattels and Credits of the said WILLIAM or unto the hands or possession of any other person or persons for him and the same so made do exhibit or cause to be exhibited into the County Court of Fairfax at such time as he shall be thereto required by the Court and the same Goods Chattels and Credits and all other the Goods Chattels and Credits of the said Deceased at the time of his Death or which at any time after shall come to the hands or possession of the said WILLIAM or into the hands or possession of any other person or persons do well and truly administer according to Law and further do make a just and true account of his actings and doings therein when thereto required by the said Court and all the rest and residue of the said Goods Chattels and Credits which shall be found remaining upon the said Admrs. account the same being examined and allowed by the Justices of the Court for the time being shall deliver and pay unto such person or persons respectively as the said Justices by their order or Judgment shall direct pursuant to the Law in that case made and provided and if is shall hereafter appear that any last Will and Testament was made by the said deceased and the executor or executors therein named do exhibit the same into the said Court making request to have it allowed and approved accordingly if the said WILLIAM SENT being thereunto required do render and deliver up his Letters of Administration approbation of such Testament being first had and made in the said Court. Then this obligation to be void else to remain in full force and vertue.
Sealed and delivered in the presence of   WILLIAM X [his mark] SENT [seal]
                                             GARRARD IT [his mark] TRAMMEL [seal]
                                             WALTER ENGLISH [seal]
At a Court continued and held for Fairfax County November the 18th 1747.
WILLIAM SENT, GARRARD TRAMMELL and WALTER ENGLISH acknowledged this Bond to be their Acts and deeds and is admitted to record.
          Test   JOHN GRAHAM, Cl. Cur.

          -In the name of God Amen. I THOMAS WILLIS of Fairfax County In the Collony of Virginia being in good health of body and of sound and parfect mind and marey praise be therefore given to almighty God do make and ordain this my present Will and Testament In manner and form following that is to say first and principally I commend my soul into the hands of almighty God hoping through the merits death and passion of my Saviour Jesus Christ to have full

p.   Fairfax County Will Book 16th March 1747/8
215   and free parden and forgiveness of all my sins and to inherit everlasting life
          and my body I commit to the earth to be decently buried at the discretion of
my dear and loving wife MARY whome I made my hole and sole Executrix as followeth
first I will that my debts and funerall charges shall be paid and discharged. Item I give

devise and bequeath unto my Dear and Loving Wife MARY all my hole Estate of what kind so ever movable and unmovable within or without be the same Real or personal unto my said loving wife MARY and her heirs for ever making ordaining constituting and appointing in during her natural life and at her dear and loving brother JOHN SHARPE and his childring for ever of this my Last Will and Testament revoking and making null and void all other or former Will or Wills by me at any time heretofore made in confirmation whereof I have hereunto sett my hand and affixed my seal this sixth day of November 1746.   THOMAS WILLIS [seal]

Signed sealed and publised in the presents of us
JOHN HIGGERSON, HENRY GUNNELL, JOHN HENDERSON
At a Court held for Fairfax County March the 16th 1747.
This Last Will and Testament of THOMAS WILLIS deceased was returned to Court by MARY WILLIS the Executrix therein named who made oath thereto according to Law and being proved by the oaths of JOHN HIGGERSON, HENRY GUNNELL and JOHN HENDERSON Evidences thereto is admitted to record the said Executrix performed what is usual in such cases Certificate is granted her for obtaining a probate in due form.   Test   JOHN GRAHAM, Cl. Cur.

-January 17th 1747/8   In the name of God Amen. I JOHN DUCKER of the County of Fairfax and Parish of Truro do will and ordain this my last Will and Testament Impromise I will that all my first Debts and Funeral Charges may be paid. Then ....all my estate after the above debts are payd to MICHAEL SKINNER in Westmoreland Count son to JOHN SKINNER in King George County to him and his heirs for ever Lastly I leave Mr. GARRARD TRAMMEL my whole and sold Executor .

JOHN HUNTER witness   JOHN P [his mark] DUCKER [seal]
WILLIAM X [his mark] HARLE
At a Court held for Fairfax County March the 16th 1747/8.
The last Will and Testament of JOHN DUCKER was proved in Court by GARRARD TRAMMEL the Executor therein named who made oath thereto and being proved by the oath of WILLIAM HARLE one of the Evidences thereto who declared he saw JOHN HUNTER the other witness subscribe the same is admitted to record and the said Executor having performed what is usual in such cases Certificate is granted him for obtaining a probate in due form.   Test   JOHN GRAHAM, Cl. Cur.

-An Appraisment of the Estate of JOHN DUCKER late of Truro Parish in the County of Fairfax in Virginia deceased schoolmaster

One horse bridle and saddle		£1.13.6

p.	Fairfax County Will Book 16th March 1747/8	
216	One suit of clothes blue grey	2.0.0
	One suit of clothes	0.15.0
	One old coat and waste coat	0.2.6
	Two linnen waste coats and old pr. of breeches	0.12.0
	Two pair of Cheqd. Trouzers	0.8.0
	Five white shirts	1.15.0
	One and a quarter of fine cloath and trimmings	0.12.0
	One yard and half brown Holland	0.3.0

Two old handchfs and bands	0.2.6
Six pr. old stockings	0.12.0
One pair ...	0.3.0
One old pewter.........	0.12.0
A knife and clothes brush	0.1.6
Three small vials	0.0.3
One shirt	0.5.0
One ditto	0.1.0
One pair stockings	0.1.0
One pair of silver lace	0.2.0
One book and others	0.1.6
One parcel old books	0.1.3
One pair gold buttons	0.19.1
Two old gold ring	0.16.0
One pair of silver clasps	0.6.0
Cash	0.12.9
One wallet with sundry trifles	<u>0.2.6</u>
	£13.5.7

Appraisers JAMES DONALDSON, ABRAHAM LAY, WILLIAM H [his mark] HARLE.
At a Court continued and held for Fairfax County March 19th 1747/8.
This Inventory and appraisement of the Estate of JOHN DUCKER was returned and
admitted to record.　　　　Test　　JOHN GRAHAM, Cl. Cur.

　　　-In Obedience to an order of Court dated the 17th November 1747.
We the subscribers being first sworn before WILLIAM SEAYRE, Gent. have valued and
apraised all and singular the Estate of JOHN EVANS deceased shown to us the apprs.
as followeth.

To 27 young hogs	3.7.6	To a parsill of old woodenware	0.3.0
To 7 sows and a bore	2.2.0	To 1 old washing tubb & old pail	0.2.0
To 1 breeding mare and colt	1.10.0	To 3 old piggins and 5 nogins	0.3.0
To 1 old horse	1.15.0	To 1 dyd woodin plates	0.2.0
To 1 ditto	3.0.0	To 7 old chears	0.6.6

p.　　　Fairfax County Will Book 16th March 1747/8

217	To 1 old ditto	2.10.0	To 1 Taylers goos and shears	<u>0.2.0</u>
	To 1 young ditto	4.0.0		57.4.6
To 6 sheep at 5/6		1.13.0	To 1 old sadel	1.10.0
To 3 cows and 3 yearlings		4.10.0	To 1 old ditto	0.6.0
To 3 cows and calves		4.0.0	To a parsell of plowing gare	0.2.6
To 1 ditto and yearling		1.5.0	To 6 sidir of leather	1.4.0
To 4 young cattell		2.0.0	To 2 deare skins	0.2.6
To 2 young styare		1.5.0	To 3 old formes and 2 old baskits	0.1.0
To 1 cow		1.10.0	To 1 old box iron and 2 heters	0.1.0
To 1 large styare		2.0.0	To 1 case of knives and forks	0.2.6
To 1 young ditto and hifer		1.5.0	To 1 case of razors and hone	0.2.0
To 2 young hifers and			To 1 old iron pott rack	0.3.0
	2 styares	2.0.0	To 1 spiel morter and pesell	0.5.0

To 1 bed and furniture	4.0.0	To 1 pair old stillards	0.1.0
To 1 ditto without fethers	1.10.0	To 1 servant man named	6.0.0
To 1 ditto and firniture	4.10.0	JOHN MURPHEY	
To 1 old chaff ditto	0.2.6	To 1 ditto named GEORGE	1.10.0
To 10 glass bottles	0.2.6	WIGHT 3 month to serve	
To 1 old spining wheall	0.6.0	To 1 servant woman named	4.0.0
To 46# puter at 8.0.0	1.9.0	MARY ROLDSON	
To a case of pistells	1.5.0	To 1 set of tea ware	0.3.0
To sum trupers arme	0.1.0	To 1 doz. earthen plates	0.1.6
To 1 sord and belt	0.5.0	To 4 old sticks	0.2.0
To 2 old tables	0.5.0	To 2 canisters	0.0.6
To 1 tin kittle	0.3.0	To 2 glass salts	0.0.2
To 3 torn wedges	1.10.0	To 2 pr. bells	0.2.0
To 1 pr. old carte wheales	0.15.0	To 3 piggs	0.0.6
To 1 narrow ax	0.5.0	To 1 turn culluder	0.1.0
To 3 old ditto and 1 hatchet	0.3.0	To 1 tankard and musterd pott	0.2.0
To 4 old grubing hoes	0.4.0	To 1 tinn pan and 3 tinn sase pans	0.1.6
To 4 old hitting ditto	0.3.0	To 1 peper box and funel	0.0.6
To 4 old weeding ditto	0.4.0	To 1 iron pott and hooks and flesh hooks	0.5.0
To 1 plow and brake	0.5.0	To 1 ditto and hooks	0.6.0
To 1 old straw bed and		To 1 large ditto and hooks	0.10.0
furniture	0.5.0	To 3 perrey wiggs	0.5.0
To 1 old blanket	0.1.0	To a parcell of waring clouaths	0.10.0
To 1 old handsaw and hamer	0.2.0	To one old quilt	0.5.0
To 6 earthen pans	0.3.0	To 1 old gun	0.8.0
To 2 pair old fire tongs	0.4.0	To 3 jacket patorns	0.15.0
To 1 old frying pan	0.2.0	To 1 old pair boots	0.2.6
To a parsell of old coopers		JOHN SUMMERS	20.11.2
Tools	0.5.0	WILLIAM DULIN	57.4.6
To 1 old carpenders adze	0.1.0	JAMES HAMILTON	77.16.8

p. __Fairfax County Will Book 16th March 1747/8__

218 At a Court continued and held for Fairfax County March the 16th 1747.

This Inventory and appraisement of the Estate of JOHN EVANS deceased was returned and admitted to record.   Test   JOHN GRAHAM, Cl. Cur.

-Pursuant to an order of Fairfax Cort dated the 18th of November 1747. We the subscribers being first sworn before LEWIS ELLZEY, Gent. one of his Majesties justices for the County aforesaid have appraised and in currant money and inventored all and singular the Estate of DAVID JONES deceased as was presented to our view as followeth

	£.S.D
To 1 grine stone 3/ 2 small cask 1/	0.4.0
To 1 bed and furniture	1.5.0
To 1 ditto 10s one chest 6/	0.16.0
To 2 iron potts and fying pan 8/ a persel of puther	0.11.0
To a persel of old lumber ½ hoes and 1 ax 3/	0.4.0
To 1 pale and 2 piggins 1 tub 6/ a persal books	0.6.0

To 1 old table and 4 stools   0.2.6

To 1 old horse and a small heiffer   <u>1.10.0</u>

December 21st 1747   JOSHUA FARGUSON   5.6.6

                               BENONI HALLEY

                               WILLIAM KITCHEN

At a Court continued and held for Fairfax County March the 16th 1747.
This Inventory and appraisement of the Estate of DAVID JONES deceased was returned and admitted to record.   Test   JOHN GRAHAM, Cl. Cur.

January the 6th 1747/8   £.S.D

To a grind stone   0.3.2

To 1 tub   0.1.2

To 2 ....and furniture   0.17.0

To 1 chest   0.6.0

To 2 pots and frying pan   0.0.6

To a parcill of puther   0.3.6

To a parcell of old lumber   0.1.3

To a barrell of old iron   0.4.1

To 1 pale 2 piggins and old parcell of books   0.6.6

To 1 table and 4 stools   0.3.3

To 1 young heifer   0.10.3

To 1 horse   <u>0.13.2</u>

                                     5.17.10

At a Court continued and held for Fairfax County March 16th 1747.
This Sale of the goods of the Estate of DAVID JONES deced. was on the motion of the Administrator admitted to record.   Test   JOHN GRAHAM, Cl. Cur.

p.   <u>Fairfax County Will Book 16th March 1747/8</u>

219   -The Estate of Mr. ZEPA. WADE deced.   Cr.

To a protested Bill of Excha. Pd. Col. BLACKBURN
        for HENRY THRELKELD   74.15.5

10 per cent on ditto 12 Mos.   7.9.6

To charge of protest 5/7d 25 percent on principal
        Protest and interest   <u>20.18</u> £103.3.6

2 To a protested Bill pd. CHRIS. LOUNDS 10 percent   10.18.7

        18 mos. 1.12.9 protest 4/3d   <u>1.17.0</u> 17.4.11 3/4

3 To a protested Bill pd. RICHARD LEE, esq.   6.0.0

        15 percent 18/ protest 4/3   <u>1.2.3</u> 9.11.11 3/4

4   To Bal. Of Bill of Exetra. Pd. THOMAS MARSHALL   8.7.5 ½ 11.6.1

5   To pd. IGNATIOUIS WHEELER per Judgt. Bond   33.15.10

6   To WILLIAM EILBECK per note of hand   10.0.0

7   To paid JOHN SKINNER per note of hand   19.0.0

8   To JAMES WIATT per note of hand   1.19.1 1/2

9   To 2700 of Tob. per JOHN DAWSON per note of hand   11.3.0

10 To paid RICHARD OSBORN per note of hand   12.0.0

11 To ditto paid OSBORN for JAMES LYRLEYS hireling
        Wages acct. Proved   3.0.0

12 To 700# Tob. per HENRY   at 10 percent   3.15.0

13 To Mr. DANIEL FRENCH, Junior per acct. Proved 40.0.0
14 To JOHN BEALL, Junior 8.1.10
15 To 805# tob. to HENRY TERRELL 4.0.6
16 To pd. YOKELEYS Exrs. note of hand
    10.3.5 1/2
17 To pd. THOMAS LEWIS per judg. 163# tob and 15/ 1.11.3
18 To JOHN MOSS pd. Judg. 552# tob and 12/6 3.9.0
19 To ROBERT WORTHINGTON bans and interest 21.10.0
20 To Quit Rents 0.8.9
21 To 1111# tob. per THOMAS WREN 5.11.1
22 To WILLIAM RAMSAY 1200# tob. at 12 percent and 16/ cash 8.7.0
23 To HENRY MASSEY, Exrs. Bills and Letters   £22.8.2 ½   22.8.8 1/2
24 To a protested Bill to ELIZ. SPENCER with costs 26.0.0
    40.18.11
25 To LEWIS NEAL assignmt. of RUTLIGE note 11.0.0
26 To RICHARD SHORES Bond with interest at 25 per cent 31.5.3
27 To Capt. JOHN WEST judget. And costs 1.17.2
28 To DAVID VANCES judgmet. 11.0.0
    457.13.7
29 To ROBERT JOHNSON per judgment. 0.11.9

p.
220

Fairfax County Will Book 16th March 1747/8
30 To WILLIAM RAMSAY for Costs 1.2.2
30 To Sundry as per account 35.2.0
    494.9.6
Remains Unsettled 230.13.11
Cr 725.3.5
By Sundrys bought by DANIEL FRENCH, Junior 40.7.0
By ditto by GEORGE JOHNSON 27.6.9
By ditto by JOHN STURMAN on acct. By GEORGE JOHNSON 5.16.8
By ditto by HENRY BELDING on acct. Ditto 0.3.0
By ditto by DANIEL HART 9.11.6
By ditto by DAVID VANCE 19.5.0
By ditto by LEWIS NEALE 5.10.0
By ditto by Maj. WASHINGTON 87.0.6
By ditto by the Admrs. 195.14.3
By one cow and heifer killed for you 2.0.0
By sundrys bought by JOHN JARVIS 2.16.0
By ditto on THOMAS MARSHALL 40.9.9
By ditto on GEORGE HENSON 13.20.6
By ditto WILLIAM RAMSAY 0.3.0
By ditto by ROBERT BOGGESS 33.2.26
By ditto by JAMES HAMILTON 1.0.0
By ditto by HUGH WEST 0.10.0
By ditto by HENRY BELDING 1.6.0
By ditto by ROBERT KING 4.14.6
By ditto by Capt. OSBORN 17.10.0

By ditto by BAXTER DAVIS		0.15.0
By cash of DANIEL McCARTY		22.10.0
By ditto reced. of Collo. WILLIAM FAIRFAX		90.1.1
By 2 sides of meals leather		1.8.0
By 100# Tob. recd. of HENRY BELDING at 10/ & £3.6.3 cash		3.16.3 1/4
By cash recd. of Capt. OSBORN		0.9.9
By ditto recd. of WILLIAM PORTER		3.14.6
By 400# Tob. recd. of Capt. HARRISON at 10/		2.0.0

p. <u>Fairfax County Will Book 16th March 1747/8</u>

221	By 2887# Tob. left by the decd. on the Plantation at 12/6	18.1.1
	By 1499# Tob. of SARAH LITTLETON at 13/	2.9.10
	By Cash Recd. of ditto	1.9.10 1/2
	By ditto Recd. of ELESAND JONES	1.0.0
	By 1500# Maryland Tob. at 8/4	6.5.0
	By 3028# ditto at ditto	12.12.4 1/2
	By 1500# ditto at ditto	<u>6.5.0</u>
		725.3.5

Dr.	Estate	
To Admrs. for Comp. On 725.3.5 at 10 percent		13.10.0
To the profits of the Mill and Miller 15 M. And half to Major WASHINGTON		37.10.0
To old Ball. To ditto		1.6.8
To 28 head of hoggs		6.11.0
To 5 M. 8d nailes		9.15.0
To Lawyers fee		2.0.0
To 1 horse		1.0.0
To iron sold JARVIS		<u>1.17.6</u>
		95.10.2
To 15 percent on £2.4.0 ster 12.6.0		<u>15.7.6</u>
		110.17.8

Feb. 8th 1747.　　　　We the Subscribers appointed to audit the account of ZEP. WADE deceased have done it within and above dated.　　RICHARD OSBORN
　　　　　　　　　　　　　　　　　　　　　　　　　　　　　　　　　JOHN WEST
　　　　　　　　　　　　　　　　　　　　　　　　　　　　　　　　　JOHN STURMAN

At a Court continued and held for Fairfax County the 16th March 1747/8. VALINDA WADE Administrix of ZEPHANIAH WADE deceased exhibited the above account against the decedents Estate and made oath thereto and the several vouchers being seen and inspected is allowed of and admitted to record.
　　　　Test　　　　　　JOHN GRAHAM, Cl. Cur.

-Dr.　　　　　The Estate of WILLIAM BURSTON, deceased		Currency
1 To JOHN GIST per Judgm.	24# Tob.	£0.11.11 1/2
2 To JOHN PETERS per acct.		0.6.6
3 To Doct. JOHN ROBERTSON per acct.		0.10.0
4 To Mr. HUGH WEST per acct.		0.5.0
5 To RICHARD STURMAN per acct.	73# Tob.	

6 To JAMES JARVIS per acct.   0.5.3

p.   Fairfax County Will Book 16th March 1747/8
222 7 To JOHN CAVENDER per acct.   0.19.8
      8 To ROBERT BOGGESS per acct.   1.18.6
      9 To ELIAS GIST per promisory note   1.6.10
      10 To Mr. THOMAS SMITH per acct.   0.5.0
      11 To JAMES HAMILTON per acct.   1.15.1 1/2
      12 To Major COCKE Cks. Note   32# Tob.
      13 To SARAH LITTLETON per acct.   0.16.6
      To 3 appraisers 2 days at 60# per   180#
      To 1 yr. Rent   Crop Tob.   500
      14 To Cash   0.1.0
      To Funeral charges   3.0.0
                       809   11.16.4
      To 1 saw sold as BURSTON's Estate claimed per
          Maj. WASHINGTON   0.13.0
      15 To Capt. RICHARD OSBORN per his acct. 0.10.0
                       809   12.19.4
      March the 16th 1747 New Ball. Due £8.9.1   0.7.1
                            £24.10.10
      March the 15th 1747 errors excepted per HENRY TREN Administrator

                            Cr.   Currency
      By the whole sale of WILLIAM BURSTON's Estate 28.3.3
      By Major LAWRENCE WASHINGTON   0.72.7
      By Capt. RICHARD OSBORN   0.9.0
                               29.4.10
      By THOMAS BOSLEY   0.12.6
      By 1 hammer iron rings 12d   0.1.6
                               29.18.10

At a Court continued and held for Fairfax County March the 16th 1748.
HENRY TRENN Administrator of WILLIAM BURSTON deceased exhibited this account against the said Decedents Estate on oath which is allowed of and admitted to record and the Tobacco vallued at 12/6 per cent.   Test   JOHN GRAHAM, Cl. Cur.

p.   Fairfax County Will Book 16th March 1747/8
223 -1747 The Estate of THOMAS ELLEZY Deced.   Dr.
      No.1 Clks. Fees   120   By the Crop of Tobacco   2771
      2 To Secretarys ditto   32   By his share of the Crop as
      3 To paid Capt. OSBORN per note 139   an overseer per
      4 To paid HUGH WEST proven acct. 0.16.7 1/4   Mr. McCARTY   1364
      5 To pd. Mr. ? per acct.   81 0.7.7   4135
      6 To pd. Mr. PAYNE per   392   By the amt. Of the Inventory
      7 To paid THOMAS MASON for note 630 By the above Tob. 4135 at
      8 To pd. CHARLES   0.16.0   10.20.3
      9. To pd.   4.1.1
      10 To paid WILLIAM YOUNG per acct.0.1.1

11 To paid WILLIAM	50	
12 To funeral expenses	1.20.6	
13 To paid WILLIAM WRIGHT	100	
14 To paid Capt. ELLEZY	333	7.14.9
15 To pailing his grave	2379	0.5.0
To the above Tobacco 2379 at 10 per		12.17.10
		24.12.10
To JOHN BROWN per note		1.2.0
		25.14.10

Errors excepted per BENONI HALLEY and MARY his wife Admrs.
At a Court continued and held for Fairfax County March the 16th 1747/8.
BENONI HALLEY and MARY his wife Admrs. of THOMAS ELLEZY deceased exhibited this account against the said Decedents Estate on oath which is allowed of and admitted to record and the Tobacco vallued at 12/6 per cent.
    Test   JOHN GRAHAM, Cl. Cur.

-April the 27th 1747

To paid LEWIS JONES tobacco out of season 600# at 10 per	3.8.0
To 1 bowl of trumpanet	0.1.3
To 1 bushel of wheat	0.3.0
To 1 man and horse and cart 4 days at 3 per bag	0.14.0
To a man and horse a day	0.2.6
To the burying of him 500 pounds of tobacco	2.10.0
To the praisers 1 day 7 pounds of tobacco	7.66
To Captain BURNAM for bringing the order 12 pounds of tobacco	0.10.0
To Clerks fee sent 40# tobacco	0.4.0
To Secretarys ditto	3.6.6
	7.13.7
To within account has by the amount of the Inventory	5.6.0

Errors excepted by WILLIAM SCOTT Admr.

p.   Fairfax County Will Book 16th March 1747/8
224   At a Court continued and held for Fairfax County March 16th 1747/8.
    WILLIAM SCOTT Admr. of DAVID JONES exhibited this account against the decedents Estate which is allowed of by the Court and admitted to record.
        Test   JOHN GRAHAM, Cl. Cur.

-A Supplementary Inventory of the Estate of Mr. ZEPH. WADE Sept. 10th 1746.
To 1 silver   3.10.0
To 3 pairs shoes
To 3 [unreadable]
To hoggs   Most of this inventory was too light to read
            RICHARD OSBORN, JOHN MANLEY
At a Court continued and held for Fairfax County March 16th 1747.
This supplementary Inventory of the Estate of ZEPH. WADE deceased was allowed and admitted to record.   Test   JOHN GRAHAM, Cl. Cur.

-Know all men by these presents that We VALINDA WADE and LAWRENCE WASHINGTON are held and firmly bound unto JOHN COLVILL, Gent. first Justice in Commission of the peace for Fairfax County for and in behalf and to the sole use and behoof of the Justices of the said County and their Successors in the sum of two hundred pounds sterling to be paid to the said JOHN COLVILL his Executors Administrators and assigns to which payment well and truly to be made we bind ourselves and every of us our and every of our heirs Executors and Administrators jointly and severally firmly by these presents sealed with our seals dated this 15th day of March Anno Domo. 1747.

The Condition of this Obligation is such that if the above bound VALINDA WADE Admrx. of the last Will and Testament of ZEPHANIAH WADE deceased thereunto annexed do make or cause to be made a true and perfect Inventory of all and singular the Goods Chattels and Credits of the said deceased which have or shall come to the hands possession or knowledge of the said VALINDA or unto the hands or possession of any other person or persons for her and the same so made do exhibit or cause to be exhibited into the County Court of Fairfax at such time as she shall be thereto required by the Court and the same Goods Chattels and Credits and all other the Goods Chattels and Credits of the said VALINDA or unto the hands or possession of any other person or persons for her and the same so made do exhibit or cause to be exhibited into the County Court of Fairfax at such time as she shall be thereto required by the Court and the same Goods Chattels and Credits and all other the Goods Chattels and Credits of the said Deceased at the time of his Death or which at any time after shall come to the hands or possession of the said VALINDA or into the hands or possession of any other person or persons do well and truly administer according to Law and further do make a just and true account of his actings and doings therein when thereto required by the said Court and all the rest and residue of the said Goods Chattels and Credits which shall be found remaining upon the said Administrators account the same being examined

p.   Fairfax County Will Book 16th March 1747/8

225   and allowed by the Justices of the Court for the time being shall deliver and pay unto such person or persons respectively as the said Justices by their order or Judgment shall direct pursuant to the Law in that case made and provided and if is shall hereafter appear that any last Will and Testament was made by the said deceased and the executor or executors therein named do exhibit the same into the said Court making request to have it allowed and approved accordingly if the said VALINDA being thereunto required do render and deliver up her Letters of Administration approbation of such Testament being first had and made in the said Court. Then this obligation to be void else to remain in full force and vertue.

Sealed and delivered in the presence of   VALINDA O [her mark] WADE [seal]
                                            LAWRENCE WASHINGTON [seal]

At a Court continued and held for Fairfax County March the 15th 1747/8.
VALINDA WADE and LAWRENCE WASHINGTON, Gent. acknowledged this Bond to be their Acts and deeds and is admitted to record.   Test   JOHN GRAHAM, Cl. Cur.

-Know all men by these presents that we GARRARD TRAMMELL and BENJAMIN SEBASTIAN are held and firmly bound unto JOHN COLVILL, Gent. first

Justice in Commission of the peace for Fairfax County for and in behalf and to the sole use and behoof of the Justices of the said County and their Successors in the sum of fifty pounds current money of Virginia to be paid to the said JOHN COLVILL his Executors Administrators and assigns to which payment well and truly to be made we bind ourselves and every of us our and every of our heirs Executors and Administrators jointly and severally firmly by these presents sealed with our seals dated this fifteenth day of March Anno Domo. 1747.

The Condition of this Obligation is such that if the above bound GARRARD TRAMMELL Admr. of the last Will and Testament of JOHN DUCKER deceased thereunto annexed do make or cause to be made a true and perfect Inventory of all and singular the Goods Chattels and Credits of the said deceased which have or shall come to the hands possession or knowledge of the said GERRARD or unto the hands or possession of any other person or persons for him and the same so made do exhibit or cause to be exhibited into the County Court of Fairfax at such time as he shall be thereto required by the Court and the same Goods Chattels and Credits and all other the Goods Chattels and Credits of the said deceased at the time of his death or which at any time after shall come to the hands or possession of the said GERRARD or into the hands or possession of any other person or

p.   Fairfax County Will Book 16th March 1747/8

226   persons for him and do well and truly administer according to Law and further
       do make a just and true account of his actings and doings therein when
thereto required by the said Court and also do well and truly pay and deliver all the Legacies contained and specified in the said Testaments as far as the said Goods Chattels and Credits will thereunto extend and the Law shall charge him then
 Then this obligation to be void else to remain in full force and vertue.
Sealed and delivered in the presence of   GERRARD IT [his mark] TRAMMELL [seal]
                                            BENJAMIN SEBASTIAN [seal]
At a Court continued and held for Fairfax County March the 16th 1747/8.
GARRARD TRAMMELL and BENJAMIN SEBASTIAN, Gent. acknowledged this Bond to be their Acts and deeds and is admitted to record. Test   JOHN GRAHAM, Cl. Cur.

       −Know all men by these presents that we SARAH LUCAS, JOHN SUMMER and WILLIAM SCOTT are held and firmly bound unto JOHN COLVILL, Gent. first Justice in Commission of the peace for Fairfax County for and in behalf and to the sole use and behoof of the Justices of the said County and their Successors in the sum of one hundred pounds to be paid to the said JOHN COLVILL his Executors Administrators and assigns to which payment well and truly to be made we bind ourselves and every of us our and every of our heirs Executors and Administrators jointly and severally firmly by these presents sealed with our seals dated this fifteenth day of March Anno Dom. 1747.

The Condition of this Obligation is such that if the above bound SARAH LUCAS Admrx. of all the Goods Chattels and Credits of JACOB LUCAS deceased do make or cause to be made a true and perfect Inventory of all and singular the Goods Chattels and Credits of the said deceased which have or shall come to the hands possession or knowledge of the said SARAH or unto the hands or possession of any other person or persons for her and the same so made do exhibit or cause to be exhibited into the

County Court of Fairfax at such time as she shall be thereto required by the Court and the same Goods Chattels and Credits and all other the Goods Chattels and Credits of the said deceased at the time of his death or which at any time after shall come to the hands or possession of the said SARAH or into the hands or possession of any other person or persons for him do well and truly administer according to Law and further do make a just and true account of his actings and doings therein when thereto required by the said Court and all the rest and residue of the said Goods Chattels and Credits which shall be found remaining upon the said Administrators account the same being first examined and allowed by the Justices of the Court for the time being shall deliver and pay unto such person or persons respectively as the said Justices by their order or judgment shall direct pursuant to the Law in that case made and provided and if it shall hereafter appear that any Last Will and Testament was made by the said deceased and the Executor or Executors

p.   Fairfax County Will Book 16th March 1747/8
227   therein named do exhibit the same in the said court making request to have it
       allowed and approved accordingly if the said SARAH being thereto required do
render and deliver up her Letters of Administration approbation of such Testament being first had and made in the said Court then this Obligation to be void else to remain in full force and vertue.
Sealed and delivered in the presence of   SARAH O [her mark] LUCAS [seal]
                                             JOHN E [his mark] SUMERS [seal]
                                             WILLIAM V [his mark] SCOTT
At a Court continued and held for Fairfax County March the 16th 1747/8.
SARAH LUCAS, JOHN SUMMERS and WILLIAM SCOTT acknowledged this Bond to be their Acts and Deeds and admitted to record.   Test   JOHN GRAHAM, Cl. Cur.

-In the name of God Amen. I EDWARD BARRY of Truro Parish and County of Fairfax being of weak body but of sound sense and memory thanks to God do make and ordain this to be my Last Will and Testament.
Imp. I bequeath my soul to God that gave it to me thro the merits of Jesus Christ for my space and joyfull resurrection and my body be interred at the discretion of my Executrix all my just debts may be paid and discharged as soon as may be after my decase and that all reasonable and just be used for the Speedy Recovery of the debts in time.
I give and bequeath unto my Loving wife MARY the lands I bought of Mr. WILLIAM GODFREY and THOMAS OWSLEY for and during her natural life and after her decease I give the said lands to my son EDWARD BARRY and to his heirs and assigns forever. I also give my said son EDWARD BARRY my negro boy DUBLIN and my negro girl HANNAH with all the future increase of said Negro girl .
I give and bequeath to my daughter ANN TILLETT one shilling sterling.
Item I give and bequeath the Tract of land bought of Capt. FRA. AWBREY Exrt. to my son JOHN BARRY and my daughter MARY BARRY and to their heirs and assigns forever and my desire is that the said tract of land may be equally divided betwixt them in quality and quantity by three honest men to be chosen for that purpose by them and that my son may have his first choice after the division so made.

Item I give and bequeath to my two daughters ELIZABETH and SARAH BARRY the tract of land I bought of JOSHUA DAVIS to be equally divided betwixt them and my will is that if all or any of my aforesaid daughters die without heirs of their bodies Lawfully begotten that the said land or lands given too them so dying shall fall and defend to my daughter MARGARET heirs and assigns forever and my intention is if my daughters ELIZABETH and SARAH have lawfull heirs

p.   Fairfax County Will Book 17th May 1748
228   of their bodys that they shall inherit the land above divided respectively.
        Item I give and bequeath the following six Negros Vizt. CASAR, HARRY, GEORGE, MINGO, BESS and BALENDA according to the appraisement of them to be equally divided between my loving wife MARY BARRY my three daughters MARY, ELIZABETH and SARAH and my son JOHN.
Item I give my daughter MARGARET BARRY and to her heirs and assigns forever my negro girl SARAH and her future increase.
Item I give and bequeath to my nephew JOHN BARRY his heirs and assigns for ever the tract of land bought from WILLIAM MOORE.
Item my will is that all my Estate not heretofore divided given and bequeathed may be equally divided between my loving wife MARY and my two sons EDWARD and JOHN and my four daughters MARY, ELIZABETH, SARAH and MARGARET BARRY.
Item since the above bequests were made I purchased a tract of land from Mr. GEORGE BYRN which tract of land I give and bequeath unto my two sons JOHN and EDWARD BARRY to them and their heirs the said land equally to be divided by three honest men by them appointed and chosen and the land so divided my son EDWARD to have the first choyce.
Lastly I bequeath constitute and appoint my Loving wife MARY BARRY to be my sole Executrix after my last Will and Testament ratifying and confirming this and disanulling all former and other Wills and Testaments of which I have hereunto set my hands and seals this 14th day of March 1747/8.
Signed Sealed and Delivered in the presence of us
        SAMUEL STONE, THOMAS x [his mark] STONE, JOHN HAMPTON
                EDWARD BARRY [seal]
At a Court held for Fairfax County May the 17th 1748.
This last Will and Testament of EDWARD BARRY deceased was presented in Court by MARY BARRY the Executrix therein named who made oath thereto according to Law and being proved by the oaths of THOMAS STONE and SAMUEL STONE who declared they see the other Evidences subscribe the same is admitted to record and the said MARY performing what is usual in such cases certificate is granted her for obtaining a probate in due form.   Test   JOHN GRAHAM, Cl. Cur.

-In the name of God Amen. JOHN TAYLOR of Fairfax County in the Colony of Virginia being very sick of body but of sound and perfect memory blessed be God doe constitute and appoint this to be my last Will and Testament revoking and disanulling all former Wills by me made if any such can be found Imprs. I bequeath my soul to God for a salvation and a joyfull Resurrection thro the Mearets of Jesus Christ. I bequeath my body to the earth from whence it came to be buried at the request. Item I bequeath to my son GEORGE

p.   <u>Fairfax County Will Book 17th May 1748</u>

228   TAYLOR one shilling having received his fortune at Marriage. Item I give and
       bequeath to my Daughter ELIZABETH SMITH one shilling having received her
fortune at Marriage. Item I give and bequeath to my son HENRY TAYLOR my negro
wench named BESS and her child and her increase to him and the heirs Lawfully
Begot of his body and in default of such heirs to return to my son GEORGE TAYLOR
and my Dorigter ELIZABETH SMITH them and their heirs forever. Item I give my son
HENRY TAYLOR one young bay horse three cows and calves one bead and furneture
four of the largest putter dishes and half a dozen putter plates five head of sheet a
table and four chairs and a pair of new cart wheals. Item I give and bequeath to my
Daughter HANNER TAYLOR a Mulatto Girl named MARY FITSGARREL also two putter
dishes and four putter plates and two young heiffers. Item Lastly after my debts fully
paid I constitute and appoint my son HENRY TAYLOR my Executor of this my last Will
and Testament as witness my hand and seal this 1st day of May 1740.

Witness   SAMPSON DARRELL   JOHN TAYLOR [seal]
               JOHN X [his mark] SHEREDIN
               JOHN I [his mark] SNODEN

At a Court held for Fairfax County May the 17th 1748.
The last Will and Testament of JOHN TAYLOR deceased presented into Court by
HENRY TAYLOR Executor therein named who made oath according to Law and being
proved by the oaths of SAMPSON DARRELL, JOHN SHEREDIN and SNODEN is
admitted to record and the Executor performing what is usual in such cases
Certificate is granted him for obtaining a probate in due form.
               Test   JOHN GRAHAM, Cl. Cur.

       -In Obedience to an order of Fairfax County dated the day of March 1747 we
the subscribers sworn before STEPHEN LEWIS, Gent. one of the Justices for the said
County as appraisers to appraise all the Estate of the deceased WILLIAM JENKINS

that was brought to our view as follows Vizt.	£.S.D
To 21 head of young hogs at	4.0.0
To 2 Large sows and two shoates at	1.0.0
To 1 cow and calf at 10s and 1 cow and yearling 20s	2.15.0
To 1 cow at 30s and ditto and yearling 40s	3.15.0
To 4 heaffers at 4s and to 2 yearlings 20s	5.0.0
To 1 old mare at 8s and young ditto at 50s	2.0.0
To 1 horse at £4 and two young mares at 50s	6.10.0
To three pair of fire tongs and a shovel and three pair of flesh forks at	0.10.6

p.   <u>Fairfax County Will Book 17th May 1748</u>

230 To 3 pair of old Taylors shears at 2s	0.2.0
To 1 box iron three ould heaters at 5s	0.5.0
To 1 ould ditto at 2s and 1 large iron spit at 5s	0.7.0
To 3 ould gimblits at 6d and a augar·at 1s	0.2.9
To pot rack at 3s and parsle old iron 15s	0.1.6
To 5 old axes at 8s and 4 wedges at 10s	0.18.0
To 1 iron pestle at 2s and 1 plow at 5s	0.10.0
To 1 grubing hoe at 2/6d and 5 heap hooks at 5s	0.7.6

To 1 drawing knife at 2s and 1 old ditto 1s	0.7.6
To 3 chisles and gouge	0.3.0
To parcel of cooper shears	0.5.6
To jointers	0.6.0
To 1 ax	0.7.6
To 1 old iron 4 poles	0.17.6
To butter poles	0.7.0
To earthen and chamber pot	0.10.0
To [unreadable]	0.6.0
To 1 old horse hide and spinning wheal	0.5.3
To 1 small cuter	0.5.6
To puter dishes	0.3.0
To a puter	0.8.0
To 1 tin funnell and 3 iron	0.2.3
To 1 ditto	0.2.6
To a parsell of earthen stone mugs at 4s	0.1.4
To stone juggs	0.2.3
To 1 puter bottle and 1 mustard pot at 6d	0.1.4
To 1 puter chamber pot at 2s 2 dozen puter spoons at 4/6d and 3 sillebub pots at 6s	0.4.0
To 1 large earthen bason and 4 earthen placks at	0.7.6
To 5 small earthen dishes at 2s	

p.
231 **Fairfax County Will Book 17th May 1748**

To 3 brown earthen porrengers at 1s	0.1.0
To 2 flowerd tumblers 1s and 1 small mugg 4d	0.1.4
To 2 scials and 3 small punch bools at 2s	0.2.0
To 1 Sarvt. Man named DUNKIN CAMBILL to serve a year and 3 months	3.10.0
To 1 servant man named CORNELUS McELAIN to serve two years 3 months	6.0.0
To 1 old skimmer and ladle at 1s	0.1.0
To 8 cheers at 14/ and 6 old ditto at 6s	1.0.0
To 2 large sows and 2 shoats at 20/ and nine 6 year cask at 4s a piece	2.16.0
To 2 runicks at 3 per 6s and 1 old ditto at 6s	0.3.6
To a parcell of old tubs at 15/	0.5.0
To 2 dozen and a quart bottles at 4s	0.11.0
To 1 large ditto at 1/6	0.1.6
To 1 small box 3/ 1 old truck 2s	0.5.0
To 1 small table at 4s 1 old ditto 1s	0.5.0
To 1 old chest	0.6.0
To 1 bed 2 blankets 1 quilt 2 pillows bed stead cord and hide No. A at £5	5.10.0
To 1 old ditto and firniture No. B at 30s	1.10.0
To 1 old ditto and rugg at parcel of sheets beadstead or pittons No. C £7	7.0.0

To 1 ditto No.D at £3.10	3.10.0
To 1 old ditto No. E at £0.10	3.10.0
To 1 old ditto No. E at 15s	0.15.0
To 1 table and forme at 10s	0.10.0
To 2 old chests at 10s 2 old trunks at 4s	0.14.0
To 2 old looking glasses at 4/ 1 shugar box 2/6	0.6.6
To 1 spinning wheal at 6/1 old table 2s	0.8.0
To 3 old saddles and 1 bridle at 15s	0.15.0
To 1 riffeles gun £3	3.0.0
To 1 smooth bord ditto at 12/6	0.12.6
To 1 soard at 5/3 cases 6 rasors 1 shop and hone	0.13.0
Brought over	£33.0.0
To 1 pair shoe buckles ditto knives at 1/6	0.1.6
To 1 stock buckle at 2/ a parcel old pailes piggens	0.12.0
1 old washing tub at 10s	
To 1 coat jacket breeches and hat at	3.10.0

P.	Fairfax County Will Book 17th May 1748	
232	to 1 broad cloath coat and jacket at 20s	1.0.0
	To 1 coat jacket and breeches at 10s	0.10.0
	To 1 suit ditto at 10s	0.10.0
	To 1 old great coat and 1 old hat	0.6.0
	To 1 old coat at 3/ 1 pair mens shoes 3	0.6.6
	To 4 pair cotton £3 1 blanket	3.5.0
	To 4 pillow 1 hair brush	0.4.6
	To 4 blankets	0.14.0
	To 2 pair old cotton cords 1 pair old wheel ditto	0.4.0
	To 1 walking cane	0.0.6
	CHARLES BROADWATER	94.4.8
	WILLIAM SHORTRIDGE	
	THOMAS WREN	

At a Court held for Fairfax County May the 17th 1748.
This Inventory and appraisement of the Estate of WILLIAM JENKINS deceased was returned and admitted to record.   Test   JOHN GRAHAM, Cl. Cur.

-In Obedience to an order of Fairfax County Court March 16th 1747 we the subscribers before WILLIAM PAYNE, Gent. have valued and appraised all and singular the Estate of THOMAS WILLIS deceased offered to us by his Executor as follows.

To [unreadable]	2.0.6	To 1 old ditto and furniture	3.0.0
To 1 [unreadable]	1.10.0	To 1 old ditto	0.6.0
To 1 ditto and ditto	1.10.0	To 1 young bull	1.0.0
To 1 ditto and calf	1.15.2	To 2 tea pans	0.3.0
To 1 heifer	1.0.0	To 44 ½# puter at 1/3	2.15.7 1/2
To 1 yearling	0.5.0	To 17# old ditto at /6	0.8.6
To 1 ditto	0.6.0	To 1 brace candlestick and scimer	0.3.0
To 7 young hoggs	1.1.0	To 1 iron ditto and one puter ditto	0.2.0

To 1 mare and colt	2.10.0	and snuffers	
To 1 horse	5.0.0	To 1 driping pan and spit	0.5.0
To 1 old ditto	1.0.0	To 1 funell and canester	0.1.3
To 10 sheep at 5s	2.10.0	To 1 mustard pot and peper box	0.2.6
To 1 bed and furniture	7.0.0	To 1 spice morter and pesell	0.6.0
To 1 ditto and furniture	7.0.0	To 1 box iron and heaters	0.3.6
		To 1 old gun	0.15.0

p.
233
Fairfax County Will Book 17th May 1748

To 1 spinning wheal	0.2.0	To 3 old rundlets	0.3.9
To 1 linning ditto	0.12.0	To 2 old sifter and old sarch	0.2.0
To 1 drum	0.10.0	To 1 old bell mettel skillett	0.4.0
To 7 fillie	0.2.4	To 2 old frying pans	0.5.0
To 1 old box or drawrs	0.5.0	To 41 pott iron at 4	0.13.10
To 1 ouel table	1.5.0	To ladle and scimer	0.1.6
To 2 old trunks	0.6.0	To 1 pr. pott hooks & 1 pr.	
To 1 ditto	0.6.0	flesh hooks	0.2.0
To 1 large chist	0.12.0	To 2 pr. poll racks	0.8.0
To 7 old chears	0.8.2	To a parsell of woode ware	0.7.0
To 2 old Razxors and an		To 1 old bed with sume furniture	0.6.0
old hone	0.1.6	To 1 large bell	0.12.6
To 1 pr. of large hillards		To 1 old ditto	0.2.6
and canhook	0.16.0	To 1 large sarnent	0.8.0
To 15 of small ditto	0.10.0	To 7 old potts	0.7.0
To 1 pr. hinges and hooks	0.10.0	To 2 old ditto	0.1.0
To 6 saills	0.6.0	To a parsell of knives and forks	0.7.0
To 4 iron wedges	0.8.0	To 3 iron	0.0.10
To 1 tenant saw	0.6.0	To 2 old [unreadable]	0.3.0
To 3 new hilling hoes	0.6.0	To 1 looking glass	0.5.0
To a bird coop	7.5.0	To 2 bunches and a pr. old	0.1.0
To 1 strip shears	0.1.0	Taylors shears	
To 1 sett tankers tools	0.10.0	To a parsell of earthenware glasses	0.6.0
To 1 curry comb and brush	0.1.6	To lanthorn	0.1.0
To 3 grubing hoes and 3 axes	0.12.0	To 17 glass bottles	0.2.10
To a parcel of old iron	0.10.0	To 1 buter pott	0.1.6
To 500 6# nails	0.2.0	To small earthen ditto	0.1.6
To 3 old broad hoes	0.5.0	To 1 horse whip	0.2.0
To 1 sart. Man named	6.0.0	To 2 old towels 1 table cloath	0.2.6
JOHN MUSKILL		1 old sheet	
To 1 ditto named	4.0.0	To 1 table cloth	0.4.0
FRANCES ARNING		To 2 ½ wool	0.2.6
To 1 sart. Woman named	6.0.0	Carryed over	28.7.9
SUSAN BAXTER			

p.
234
Fairfax County Will Book 17th May 1748

		76.14.7
To one old knife and fork		0.0.6

To 2 old baggs		0.2.0
To 1 pr. money skils	4/0	£76.19.1
		0.4.0
		£77.3.1
To 2 old wheat redils		0.3.0
To 2 pr. of wool cords and 1 pare of cotton cardes		0.3.0
To 3 sows and a barrow		1.0.0
To 2 ditto		0.7.6
To 4 piggs		0.4.0
To parsel of iron		0.1.0
To [unreadable]		0.1.6
		79.3.1
To 18 yds. of country linnen		1.2.6
To 10 yrds. Thread		0.10.5
		1.42.55
		00.15.0
		00.15.0

WILLIAM PAYNE, HENRY GUNNELL, Junior, JAMES HAMILTON, WILLIAM SCOTT
At a Court held for Fairfax County the 17th day of May 1748.
This Inventory and appraisment of the Estate of THOMAS WILLIS deceased was returned and admitted to record.   Test   JOHN GRAHAM, Cl. Cur.

-Fairfax County 30th day 1748	£.S.D
To [unreadable]	1.10.6
To [unreadable]	2.0.0
To [unreadable]	1.15.0
To two cows and three yearlings	4.0.0
To two heifers and young stear	3.0.0
To 1 young mare	0.15.0
To one old horse	1.0.0
To one old and furniture	2.0.0
To one old bed and bed cloths and hide	1.0.0
To one spinning wheal	0.7.0
To one old and box and two tables	0.11.0
To one old puter tankard	0.2.0
To sixteen pound and a half of puter	0.16.6

p. 235	Fairfax County Will Book 17th May 1748	
	To fourteen pounds of old puter	0.8.2
	To a parsell of wooden wear and some old lumber	0.5.0
	To one sarch and sifter att	0.4.0
	To one box iron and heaters att	0.1.0
	To one persel of earthen wear	0.5.0
	To one brass candle stick one tin peper box and fonal	0.5.0
	To three quart bottles att	0.1.10
	To thirty six pound and a quart of pott iron	0.0.6

To two pair of pott hooks att	0.9.0
To 2 wedges and a persal of old iron	0.1.6
To one hansay at	0.5.0
To one frying pan at	0.2.6
To one small bible att	0.0.6
To two old chairs att	0.2.0
To a parsell of old cloaths att	0.8.0
MICHAEL REAGAN, JOHN MOSS, ROGER WIGGINTON	£22.5.4

At a Court held for Fairfax County the 17th day of May 1748.
This Inventory and appraisement of the Estate of JACOB LUCAS deceased was returned and admitted to record.   Test   JOHN GRAHAM, Cl. Cur.

-Dr. The Estate of ZEPH. WADE deceased	
To [unreadable]	1.3.3
2 To [unreadable]	1.21.6
3 To [unreadable]	49.2.6
4 To paid ROBERT BURGIS to money lent as was proved	14.0.2 1/2
5 To paid WILLIAM EILIEBECK per account proved	1.8.0
6 To paid ditto as per ditto £36.18.1 at 25 per	4.17.6
7 To paid WILLIAM RAMSAY 29	18.13.7 1/2
To paid ditto current money being part of his account	12.17.0
To sundrys as was in the Mill which was appraised and	
Belonged to Major WASHINGTON amounting to	13.0.5
To Mr. JOHN PAGAN 4812 # tobacco at 12/6 £35.1.6	135.1.0
To ditto in account 4.15.6	

p.   Fairfax County Will Book 17th May 1748
236

10 To JOHN SHERMON Attorneayes	9.5.0
11To paid EDMUND JENINGS, Esq. to appear to	
Ann account by Major LAWRENCE WASHINGTON	2.10.0
12 To 345# Tob. CLARKES at 10 percent	1.14.0
To 40 days the Estate has the Mill longer then the	3.6.8
Admr. At 20 per day which was omited in the account	
Settled with the Court	
To Admr. for Comp. On £46.10.8 at 6 percent	2.15.0
	172.0.4
To paid JOHN KING by recd. 21# Tob. at 10 percent	0.2.1 ¼
To 17 days work at 13 per day	
To shelling and bringing [unreadable]	1.0.0
The remainder of the page is too light to read easily	

At a Court held for Fairfax County May the 17th 1748.
VALINDA WADE account of the last Will and Testament of ZEPH. WADE was returned and admitted to record.   Test   JOHN GRAHAM, Cl. Cur.

-1747 THOMAS SCANLING, Deced.			
To one cotten	0.7.6	To digging a grave	2.2.6
To one sheet	0.9.0	To loging the grave in	0.2.6

98

p.   Fairfax County Will Book 18th May 1748

237	To stripping the corps	0.3.0	To pasturidge for my horse	0.6.0
	To horse hire	0.3.0	To shipping packing and pursing	
	To provisions	0.4.6	and carrying to the warehouse	
	To ditto at another time	0.1.3	2 hhd Tobacco	1.10.0
	To boarding myself 10 days	0.7.6	To getting up the stock to be	
	To 3 men praysing one day		praised	0.10.0
	One day Tob. 90#	4.6.9		

Errors excepted per JANE SCANLING Administratrix

At a Court continued and held for Fairfax County May the 18th 1748.
JANE SCANLING, Admrx. of THOMAS SCANLING, Exhibited this account against the decease and made oath thereto which was allowed and admitted to record and the Tobacco valued at 12/6 percent.   Test   JOHN GRAHAM, Cl. Cur.

-To one mare of the Estate of JOHN LITTLETON praised to
praised by JOHN MANLEY and THOMAS LEWIS.
At a Court continued and held for Fairfax County May the 18th 1748.
This additional Inventory of JOHN LITTLETON deceased was returned in Court and admitted to record.   Test   JOHN GRAHAM, Cl. Cur.

-Know all men by these presents that we MARY BARRY, LEWIS ELLZEY, JOHN TURLEY, EDWARD WASHINGTON, MICHAEL REAGAN are held and firmly bound unto JOHN COLVILL, Gent. first Justice in Commission of the peace for Fairfax County for and in behalf and to the sole use and behoof of the Justices of the said County and their Successors in the sum of one thousand pounds sterling to be paid to the said JOHN COLVILL his Executors Administrators and assigns to which payment well and truly to be made we bind ourselves and every of us our and every of our heirs Executors and Administrators jointly and severally firmly by these presents sealed with our seals dated this 17th day of May 1748.
The Condition of this Obligation is such that if the above bound MARY BARRY, Extrix. of the Last Will and Testament of EDWARD BARRY deceased do make or cause to be made a true and perfect Inventory of all and singular the Goods Chattels and Credits of the said Deceased which have or shall come to the hands or possession or knowledge of the said MARY or into the hands or possession of any other person or persons for her and the same so made do exhibit or cause to be exhibited into the County Court of Fairfax at such time as she shall thereto be required by the said Court and the same Goods Chattels and Credits and all other Goods Chattels and Credits of the said Deceased at the time of his Death or which at any time after shall come to the hands or possession of the said MARY or into the hands or possession of any person or persons for her do well and truly administer according to Law and further do make a

p.   Fairfax County Will Book 18th May 1748

238   just and true account of their actings and doings therein when thereto
        required by the said Court and also do well and truly pay and deliver all the

Legacies contained and specified in the said Testament as far as the said Goods Chattels and Credits will thereunto extend and the Law shall charge her then this obligation to be void and of none effect or else to be and remain in full force and virtue.   Sealed and Delivered in presence of the Court
          MARY M [her mark] BARRY [seal]   LEWIS ELLZEY [seal]
          JOHN TURLEY [seal]   EDWARD WASHINGTON [seal]
          MICHAEL REAGAN [seal]
At a Court held for Fairfax County May the 17th 1748.
MARY BARRY, LEWIS ELLZEY, JOHN TURLEY, EDWARD WASHINGTON and MICHAEL REAGAN acknowledged this Bond to be their Acts and Deeds and admitted to record.
          Test   JOHN GRAHAM, Cl. Cur.

          -Know all men by these presents that we HENRY TAYLOR, JOHN SHERIDON and JOSEPH GARDNER are held and firmly bound unto JOHN COLVILL, Gent. first Justice in Commission of the peace for Fairfax County for and in behalf and to the sole use and behoof of the Justices of the said County and their Successors in the sum of five hundred pounds sterling to be paid to the said JOHN COLVILL his Executors Administrators and assigns to which payment well and truly to be made we bind ourselves and every of us our and every of our heirs Executors and Administrators jointly and severally firmly by these presents sealed with our seals dated this 17th day of May 1748.
The Condition of this Obligation is such that if the above bound HENRY TAYLOR Executor of the Last Will and Testament of JOHN TAYLOR deceased do make or cause to be made a true and perfect Inventory of all and singular the Goods Chattels and Credits of the said Deceased which have or shall come to the hands or possession or knowledge of the said HENRY or into the hands or possession of any other person or persons for him and the same so made do exhibit or cause to be exhibited into the County Court of Fairfax at such time as he shall thereto be required by the said Court and the same Goods Chattels and Credits and all other Goods Chattels and Credits of the said Deceased at the time of his Death or which at any time after shall come to the hands or possession of the said HENRY or into the hands or possession of any person or persons for him do well and truly administer according to Law and further do make a just and true account of their actings and doings therein when required by the said Court and also do well and truly pay and deliver all the Legacies contained and specified in the said Testament as farr as the said Goods Chattels

p.   Fairfax County Will Book 18th May 1748
239   and Credits will thereunto extend and the Law shall charge him then this
       Obligation to be void and of none effect or else to remain in full force and
virtue.   Sealed and Delivered in the presence of
          HENRY TAYLOR [seal]   JOHN I [his mark] SHERIDON [seal]
          JOSEPH GARDNER [seal]
At a Court held for Fairfax County May the 18th 1748.
HENRY TAYLOR, JOHN SHERIDON and JOSEPH GARDNER acknowledged this Bond to be their Acts and Deeds and admitted to record.   Test   JOHN GRAHAM, Cl. Cur.

-Know all men by these presents that we JOHN CARLYLE and BENJAMIN SEBASTIAN are held and firmly bound unto the worshipfull Justices of Fairfax County in the sum of one hundred pounds to be paid to the said Justices theirs heirs and Successors to which payment well and truly to be made we bind ourselves and every of us our and every of our heirs Executors and Administrators jointly and severally firmly by these presents sealed with our seals dated this 18th day of May Anno Dom. 1748.

The Condition of this Obligation is such that if the above bound JOHN CARLYLE Administrator of the Last Will and Testament of JOHN CHESHIRE deceased do make or cause to be made a true and perfect Inventory of all and singular the Goods Chattels and Credits of the said Deceased which have or shall come to the hands or possession or knowledge of the said JOHN or into the hands or possession of any other person or persons for him and the same so made do exhibit or cause to be exhibited into the County Court of Fairfax at such time as he shall thereto be required by the said Court and the same Goods Chattels and Credits and all other Goods Chattels and Credits of the said Deceased at the time of his Death or which at any time after shall come to the hands or possession of the said JOHN or into the hands or possession of any person or persons for him do well and truly administer according to Law and further do make a just and true account of their actings and doings therein when required by the said Court and all the rest and residue of the said account the same being first examined and allowed by the Justice of the Court for the time shall deliver and pay unto such person or persons respectively as the said Justices by them order or judgment shall direct pursuant to the laws in that case made and provided and if it shall hereafter appear that any Last Will and Testament was made by the said deceased and the Executor or Executors therein named do exhibit the same in the said Court making request to have it allowed and approved accordingly if the said JOHN CARLYLE being thereunto required do render and deliver up his Letters of Administration approbation of such Testament being first had and made in the said Court then this obligation to be void and of none effect otherwise to remain in full

p.   Fairfax County Will Book 18th May 1748
240   force and virtue. Sealed and Delivered in presence of the Court
            JOHN CARLYLE [seal]   BENJAMIN SEBASTIAN [seal]
At a Court continued and held for Fairfax County May 18th 1748.
JOHN CARLYLE and BENJAMIN SEBASTIAN acknowledged this Bond to be their Acts and Deeds and admitted to record. Test   JOHN GRAHAM, Cl. Cur.

-Know all men by these presents that we RICHARD BROWN, THOMAS CONNELL and ROBERT LINDSEY are held and firmly bound unto JOHN COLVILL the first Justice in Commission of the peace for Fairfax County for and in behalf and to the sole use and behoof of the Justices of the said County and their Successors in the sum of one hundred pounds to be paid to the said JOHN COLVILL his Executors Administrators and assigns to which payment well and truly to be made we bind ourselves and every of us our and every of our heirs Executors and Administrators jointly and severally firmly by these presents sealed with our seals dated this 21st day of June 1747.

The Condition of this Obligation is such that if the above bound RICHARD BROWN Admrx. of all the Goods Chattels and Credits of JOHN BROWN deceased do make or cause to be made a true and perfect Inventory of all and singular the Goods Chattels and Credits of the said Deceased which have or shall come to the hands or possession or knowledge of the said RICHARD or into the hands or possession of any other person or persons for him and the same so made do exhibit or cause to be exhibited into the County Court of Fairfax at such time as he shall thereto be required by the said Court and the same Goods Chattels and Credits and all other Goods Chattels and Credits of the said Deceased at the time of his Death or which at any time after shall come to the hands or possession of the said RICHARD or into the hands or possession of any person or persons for him do well and truly administer according to Law and further do make a just and true account of their actings and doings therein when required by the said Court and all the rest and residue of the said account the same being first examined and allowed by the Justice of the Court for the time shall deliver and pay unto such person or persons respectively as the said Justices by them order or judgment shall direct pursuant to the laws in that case made and provided and if it shall hereafter appear that any Last Will and Testament was made by the said deceased and the Executor or Executors therein named

p.   Fairfax County Will Book 21ˢᵗ June 1748

241   do exhibit the same into the said Court making bequest to have it allowed and approved accordingly if the said RICHARD being thereunto required do render and deliver up Letters of Administration approbation of such Testament being first had and made in the said Court then this obligation to be void and of none effect or else to remain in full force and virtue. Sealed and Delivered in the presence of

RICHARD BROWN [seal]   THOMAS CONNELL [seal]   ROBERT LINDSEY [seal]

At a Court held for Fairfax County June the 21ˢᵗ 1748.

RICHARD BROWN, THOMAS CONNELL and ROBERT LINDSEY acknowledged this Bond to be their Acts and Deeds and admitted to record.

Test   JOHN GRAHAM, Cl. Cur.

-March 26 1748   The Estate of Mr. JOHN DUCKER, deceased

To cash paid Docter JOHN HUNTER as [unreadable]	0.18.6
To cash paid Mr. JOHN BROWN as per ditto	1.1.1
To cashh paid JOSEPH GARDNER as per ditto	0.0.1
To the Lawyers fee on the Estate	0.13.0
To my trouble and attendance on him in his sickness that in days at 3/ per day	1.10.0
To funeral expense	3.0.0
To wintering his horses	0.10.0
To the Ballance of Mr. JAMES HAMILTON bill	0.32.11
To Tobacco paid Mr. JOHN PAGAN as per account proved	285
To ditto paid [unreadable]	11
To paid Mr. GARRARD ALEXANDER as per ditto crop	80
To the appraisal fee	90

To the Secretarys fee	32	
To the Clerks fee	32	
To Commission on the whole at 10/ percent	95	1.13.6
	693	£9.3.2
1748 per Contra	Cr	
By the sale of the Estate what sold		9.11.4 1/2
By Cash 12/6d		0.12.6
By one old saddle and bridle		0.12.0
By some old lumber		0.2.6
By one gould ring and one pr. of gold buttons		1.15.7
By one band clasp		0.6.0

p.   Fairfax County Will Book 21st June 1748

242 By Mr. CHARLES BROADWATER	130	
By DANIEL TRAMMEL	101	
By Mr. JAMES ROBERTSON	150	
By one large brush		0.1.0
By some old boots		0.1.3

        Errors excepted per GARRARD TRAMMELL, Executor
At a Court held for Fairfax County June the 21st 1748.
GARRARD TRAMMELL Executor of JOHN DUCKER proved his account against the
Decedents Estate and made oath thereto which allowed of by the Court and admitted
to record.   Test   JOHN GRAHAM, Cl. Cur.

-The Estate of Doctor THOMAS ARBUTHNOT	
To 4 months Maintenance of the Family Vizt. eight	£.S.D
Tenents children from the Doctor ARBUTHNOT's	30.00.0
[unreadable]	25.00.0
[unreadable] South River in Maryland	15.10.0
To paid Mr. TRAN for an obligation of Doctor	
ARBUTHNOT [unreadable]	12.0.0
To charges of Witnesses going to praise the Will	6.9.0
To Funerall charges	9.0.0
Errors excepted by MARGARET ARBUTHNOT	£97.19.0

        Hanover County Certified that this day Mrs. MARGARET ARBUTHNOT made
oath before me one of his Majesties Justices of the peace for the said County that
the above ninety seven pounds nineteen shillings just and true Certified under my
hand this 5th day of April 1745.   WILLIAM MERIWETHER

p.   Fairfax County Will Book 19th July 1748

243 Ditto BRYAN ALLISON Taylor	0.19.0
JAMES CROSBY's Account	0.16.0
CHARLES GRIFFETH account	1.1.6
.... per ..... GRAHAM	10.0.0
ARBUTHNOT [unreadable]	12.10.0
The above vouchers sent one by Mr. ARBUTHNOT	£25.6.6
Also shows accounts all but June the ditto death the him 3.2.0 paid	

By Mr. ARBUTHNOT   09.13.1
At a Court held for Fairfax County July the 19th 1748.
The account charged by MARGARET ARBUTHNOT Exrx. of THOMAS ARBUTHNOT
deceased exhibited this account against the Decedents Estate and the vouchers
being seen and inspected is acknowledged and admitted to record.
                    Test   JOHN GRAHAM, Cl. Cur.

          -Know all men by these presents that we DANIEL JAMES and EDWARD EMMS
are held and firmly bound unto JOHN COLVILL the first Justice in Commission of the
peace for Fairfax County for and in behalf and to the sole use and behoof of the
Justices of the said County and their Successors in the sum of twenty pounds to be
paid to the said JOHN COLVILL his Executors Administrators and assigns to which
payment well and truly to be made we bind ourselves and every of us our and every
of our heirs Executors and Administrators jointly and severally firmly by these
presents sealed with our seals dated this [unreadable].
The Condition of this Obligation is such that if the above bound DANIEL JAMES Admr.
of all the Goods Chattels and Credits of ROBERT DONNALY deceased do make or
cause to be made a true and perfect Inventory of all and singular the Goods Chattels
and Credits of the said Deceased which have or shall come to the hands or
possession or knowledge of the said DANIEL or into the hands or possession of any
other person or persons for him and the same so made do exhibit or cause to be
exhibited into the County Court of Fairfax at such time as he shall thereto be required
by the said Court and the same Goods Chattels and Credits and all other Goods
Chattels and Credits of the said Deceased at the time of his Death or which at any
time after shall come to the hands or possession of the said DANIEL or into the
hands or possession of any person or persons for him do well and truly administer
according to Law and further do make a just and true account of their actings and
doings therein when required by the said Court and all the rest and residue of the
said account the same being first examined and allowed by the Justice of the Court
for the time shall deliver and pay unto such person or persons respectively as the
said Justices by them order or judgment shall direct

p.   Fairfax County Will Book 18th August 1748
244   pursuant to the laws in that case made and provided and if it shall hereafter
        appear that any Last Will and Testament was made by the said deceased and
the Executor or Executors therein named do exhibit the same into the said Court
making bequest to have it allowed and approved accordingly if the said DANIEL being
thereunto required do render and deliver up Letters of Administration approbation of
such Testament being first had and made in the said Court then this obligation to be
void and of none effect or else to remain in full force and virtue.
Sealed and Delivered in the presence of   DANIEL JAMES [seal]
                                            EDWARD E [his mark] EMMS [seal]
At a Court continued and held for Fairfax County August the 18th 1748.
DANIEL JAMES and EDWARD EMMS acknowledged this Bond to be their Acts and
Deeds and admitted to record.   Test   JOHN GRAHAM, Cl. Cur.

-Pursuant to an order of the Court dated the 17th...... we the ...... and being first sworn before a Justice of the peace of this County

[the first part of this listing is very light and hard to read]

To 1 # of puter at 9d 12/ to 20 ditto at 18/4	1.10.4
To a parcel of earthen ware	1.11.0
To some old lumber	2.10.0
To 2 old chist a hunt and 2 old tables 17s to a parcel of tools and some iron	2.1.0
To 3 painted boxes and a pr. of money scales	0.5.0
To a warming pan 5s to a grub skiner candle stick 6s	0.11.0
To 1 box iron chest lock and looking glass 5s to pr. of shirts 6s	0.13.0
To a pr. of tongs pestel bell and som old iron 10	0.10.0
To 5 old chairs 5s to 8 old baskets 4s to 3 iron potts 10s to 1 iron skillet and gridel	1.1.6
To a parcel of old backs a ladel and 2 pr. of pott hooks	0.10.0

p. 245   <u>Fairfax County Will Book 18th August 1748</u>

To 2 brass kittles a morter and pestel	1.0.0
To a parcel of old hoes and 3 old axes 10/ to 1 grind stone 4/	0.14.0
To a riddel and ho3/ to a sarch and sifter 3/	0.6.0
To axes and hooks 5/ to 1 ax plough 2/	0.7.0
To part of an old sain 5/ to 3 old spinning wheals 5/	0.10.0
To half of a tact rien 6/	1.1.0
To his wairing appirril £1.10 or parcil of old books 12/	2.2.0
To 1 old hair brush	0.17.2 1/2
To the crop of Tobacco 669#	90.5.0
To 22 hoggs at 5/ pr. heifers and sow and piggs at 8/	<u>05.10.00</u>
	96.03.1/2

SAMPSON DARRELL, SAMUEL I [his mark] JOHNSON, JOHN X [his mark] CARNEY
At a Court held for Fairfax County August 18th 1748.
This Inventory and appraisement of the Estate of JOHN TAYLOR deceased was admitted to record.   Test   JOHN GRAHAM, Cl. Cur.

-Pursuant to an order of Fairfax County Court we the Subscribers being first sworn before Capt. LEWIS ELLEZY and WILLIAM PAYNE, Gent. have sworn tried and appraised all and singular the Estate of JOHN BROWN deceased which was to view Vizt.

One old horse	£1.10.0
One old gun	0.16.0
31 yards of white linnen	0.0.9
A parcel of old shirts &c	0.5.0
One cloth jackett	0.8.0
A parcel of old cloths	0.13.0
One pair of thread stockins	0.5.0
4 pair of old yard stockings	0.6.0
2 pair of old shoes	0.3.0
One razer and cuse	0.0.6

A parcel of carpenters tools	0.10.6
One old saddle bridle and horse bell	0.10.0
	£5.15.9

RICHARD SIMPSON, WILLIAM SIMPSON, JOHN BARRY } Appraisers

p.   Fairfax County Will Book 16th August 1748
246 At a Court held for Fairfax County August 16th 1748.
This Inventory and appraisement of the Estate of JOHN BROWN deced. was returned and admitted to record.   Test JOHN GRAHAM, Cl. Cur.

-JOHN BROWN, deced.

To 2 year 2 months an ½ board at 3 pr. yr.	6.12.6
To one [unreadable]	0.6.0
To [unreadable]	0.5.0
To [unreadable]	0.12.0
To 10 ditto or 6	0.2.3
To [unreadable]	0.1.3
To paid ROBERT BOGGESS	0.0.7 1/2
To paid EDWARD BARRY	0.0.6
To cash paid for wool	0.3.0
To spinning and knitting one pair of stockings	0.3.6
To one pair of [unreadable]	0.0.6
To 30# of crop tobacco at 10s per #	1.5.0
To horse	0.1.0
To expenses	1.10.0
	£11.6.8
To Mr. HUGH WEST for the year 1746	34# tobacco
To Mr. WM. ELLZEY for the year 1747	35# tobacco
Contra	Cr
By 19 days work	1.10.0
By work in my dwelling house	1.0.0
By pailing	1.5.0
By STEPHEN McMILLION	0.1.5
By 1 sheet	0.6.0
By the Inventory	5.15.9
By a pair of wooll	0.9.0
By EDWARD BARRY 200# tobacco	£10.16.7

Errors excepted per RICHARD BROWN Admr.

p.   Fairfax County Will Book 16th August 1748
247 At a Court held for Fairfax County August the 16th 1748.
RICHARD BROWN Admr. of JOHN BROWN deceased exhibited this account on oath against the decedents Estate which examined is allowed of and admitted to record.   Test   JOHN GRAHAM, Cl. Cur.

-1744	The Estate of CHARLES NEALE deceased	tobacco	cash
March to your bowls for one year		300	

To one pair leather breeches	150	
To one pair of shoes	050	
To one pair shoe buckles and old dry or never returned	012	
To plows	150	0.4.6
To tobacco reading you at Mr. PAGAN's store	065	
To cash paid THOMAS WHITFORD as per account proved		0.18.3
To cash paid BENJAMIN SEBASTIAN per account proved		1.2.6
To cash paid Ditto per receipt		0.0.6
To the Secretays and Clerks fees per the Admr. & Certificate	77	
To this Clerk and Sheriff his receipt from JAMES ROBERTSON	52	
To the appraisers	90	
	946	£2.12.9

Errors excepted per JAMES YOUNG and MARY his wife Admrs. with the witnesses of the last Will of CHARLES NEALE deceased.
At a Court held for Fairfax County August the 16th 1748.
JAMES YOUNG and MARY his wife brought this account against the Estate of CHARLES NEALE deceased which being examined is proved of by the Court and admitted to record and the Tobacco valued at 12/6 percent.
Test JOHN GRAHAM, Cl. Cur.

-In Obedience to an order of Court of the we the Subscribers being first sworn before a Justice of the peace have appraised and valued all the Estate of RICHARD POULTNEY deceased that came to our view Vizt.

1 Bed and old furniture	5.0.0
5 new plates 1 old ditto 1 dish and 1 tunnel	0.12.0
2 Bays one 5/ 1 tin pot 1 pair stillnards 8/	0.14.0
1 huckle 5/ 2 old saithes 25/ 1 iron pot 10/	2.0.0
1 large wheat 7/ 1 small ditto old 5/	0.12.0
1 horse Ingraham 3.10.1 ditto duike 6# 1 ditto pompey 40/	11.10.0
1 cutting knife and box 22/ 1 old plow shear and colter 20/	1.2.0
1 Boy THOMAS 4 1 old	10.1.0

p.
248

Fairfax County Will Book 20th September 1748

3 horse chains ½ of 4 sides of leather 2 of and currying knife 9/	1.19.0	
22 sheep 5.5 1 grey mare £3 1 colt 5d	13.5.0	
1 old bed and furniture £3.1 turkey feather ditto & 2 ruggs 30/	4.10.0	
1 bed bolster 1 rugg and 2 sheets	5.0.0	
1 old tray and ginger 4/ 1 oval table 20/	1.4.0	57.9
1 old tub and flax seed of 1 search 2/	0.5.0	
1 looking glass 4/ 4 old pilow cases	0.6.0	
7 old towells 4/ 8 old napkins	0.16.0	
2 table cloths 2/ 1 chest 1 desk	4.12.0	
1 large bell 2 table and 1 old half bushel	0.12.0	
1 old brass morter and pestel 8 bottles	0.3.6	
12 punch bowles 2 wash basons and sundry earthen ware	1.0.0	

1 copper pot 6 earthen pans and 6 polls 18s	1.8.0
A parcel of tin ware 10/ a parcel of puter	0.18.0
To 2 earthen juggs 2/ 7 old chairs 10/	0.12.0
One chease knife and 1 pair sheep shears	0.2.0
3 sides of leather 10/ 2 old tubbs and other lumber	0.14.0
10 pair shoes 3 old boxes	2.3.0
15 new spoons 3/ 1 bunch mohair 12/	0.15.0
8 pair spoons a box knives 7 knives	0.16.0
14 shoes	0.11.8
1 punch ladle 1 desk furniture	0.6.1
2 papers of Laces 15 horn books 1 primmer 1 pair of buttons	1.18.0
A parcel of buckles thimbles sleeve buttons laces cork screws and flax	0.12.0
1 old small wheets 6 pair silk	0.16.0
8 thread for string	0.5.0
1 doz. combs 3 pair sape and small buckles 3 razors	1.9.0 12.9
To sum broken wear	£80.12.8
1 iron bays	0.11.0
1 pair taylors shears 1 pair money scales	0.9.6
2 new hoes 5/ 1 old gun 10/	0.15.0
A parcel of old hoes axes and old iron 8/	0.8.0
1 servant man JOHN MIRES	5.0.0 1.13.6
8 bunches silk 6/ 1 large iron pot and hooks 1/	0.16.0
1 small pot and hooks 5/ 1 kettle and hooks 7/	0.12.0
1 large frying pan 3/ 1 brass skil as 5/	0.8.0
1 pair tongues 3/ 1 old ladle 1 gridle 2/	0.5.0
2 old piggins 1 old pale 3/ 1 pair flesh forks 2/	0.4.0
2 old tables of 1 grind stone 4/	0.7.0
1 red cow and calf 46/ 1 ditto and calf 45/	4.10.0
1 black ditto and calf 40/ 1 two year old steer 15/	2.15.0

p.
249

Fairfax County Will Book 20th September 1748

2 two year old heifers 30/ 1 roan mare and colt 50/	4.0.0
3 large young horses 4d 1 yold sorrell ditto 40/	6.0.0 19.17
1 white pyde heifer 26/ 1 ditto 1 year old 15/	2.0.0
1 brown cow and calf 33/ 1 red steer 25/	3.0.0
1 black yearling 12/ 1 dun cow and yearling 45/	2.17.0
1 black ditto & ditto 24/ 1brown ditto & ditto 40/ 1 red steer 25/ 5.10.0	
1 young brindled heifer 15/ 1 brown steer 3 0/ 1 red ditto 25/	3.10.0
1 heifer and calf 30/ 19 young hoggs and piggs 5d	6.10.0
1 boy JOHN SCOTT 4d ditto JAMES ANDERSON £3	7.0.0
1 ditto MICHAEL RUSHODE 40/ 1 plow and irons 14/	2.14.0
2 old axes 2/ 3 old hoes 6/ 1 grubbing ditto	0.9.6
1 grind stone 5/ 2 iron croked basons 4/	0.2.0
1 frying pan 2d/6 1 iron pot and hooks 4/	0.6.0
1 old broken pit 3/ 1 old bell and 2 wedges 6/	0.9.0
1 large pale 2d/6 1 old bed 2 old blankets and a mugg 5/	0.7.6

1 gun 20/ 1 fluke plow 3/ 2 hoes 8/		1.11.0
1 pair stilliards 10/ 1 box iron and heathers 5/6		0.13.6
1 brindled cow and calf 5/ 2 cross cut saw 9/		2.14.0
5 roap hooks 3d6 1 shoe hammer and 1 pair nipers		
and pinchers		0.6.0 40.11
1 black cow and brindled yearling 40/		2.5.0
1 white ditto and yearling		1.0.0 4.5
		£152.10.2

Nov. 17th 1747 Given under our hands   DAVID RICHARDSON
                                          JOHN GORDEN
                                          THOMAS AWBREY

At a Court held for Fairfax County September the 20th 1748.
This Inventory and appraisement of the Estate of RICHARD POULTNEY deceased was
this day returned and admitted to record. Test   JOHN GRAHAM, Cl. Cur.

This ends this part of the Fairfax County Will Book 1742 – 1752.
The next book will start at the bottom of page 249 with the list of items in the
Inventory of the Estate of EDWARD BARRY deceased.

ELLZEY. 26, 27; Capt. 88; Francis 18,
 19; Lewis 27, 83, 100, 105;
 Thomas 19, 87, 88; William 106.
EMMS. Edward 57, 58, 104.
ENGLISH. Edmund 7, 8, 19, 20;
 Elizabeth 7; Sarah 7, 8, 9; Walter
 7, 8, 9, 19, 76, 77, 79, 80.
EVANS. John 18, 49, 53, 55, 62, 69, 77,
 79, 82, 83 Margrat (Margaret)
 77, 79.
FAIRFAX. William 86.
FARGUSON. John 5, 7, 14; Josiah
 (Joshua) 29, 84.
FAULKNER. (FALKNER) Thomas 20,
 21, 74, 79.
FITSGARREL. Mary 93.
FLOYD. John 1, 2.
FORD. Thomas 21.
FOSTER. Robert 67.
FOUCH. Hugh 31.
FRANCIS. Martin 78.
FRENCH. Daniel 2, 7, 18, 28, 43, 68;
 Daniel Jr. 28, 84, 85.
FRY. Joseph 1.
GARDNER. Joseph 38, 39, 100, 102.
GARNER. Bradley 19.
GARRARD. William 16.
GASKIN. Mary 11.
GIBSON. John 49.
GILESSON. John 69.
GILMORE. Owen 5, 28.
GIST. Elias 87; John 74, 86.
GLADDEN/GLADING. John 57,61,65.
 71,78; William-12.
GODFREY. 35; William 7, 91.
GORDON. (GORDEN) John 11, 12, 31,
 78, 109.
GRAHAM. 103; John 65, 66, 67,
 68, 69, 70, 71, 72, 73, 74, 75, 77,
 78, 79, 80, 81, 82, 83, 84, 86, 88,
 89, 90, 91, 92, 93, 95, 97, 98, 99,
 100, 101, 102, 103, 104, 105,
 106, 107, 109.
GRAYSON. Major 35.
GREEN. 29.
GRIFFETH. Charles 103; David 17, 18.
GRIMES. 27; William 39.
GRIMWOOD. William 16, 60, 67, 68,
 71, 72.
GRINSTED. James 16.
GROVE. William 10.
GUMMERSON. 13.
GUNNELL. Henry 75, 81, 97.
GUTHRIE. James 29.
GUY. William 76.
HAGUE. Francis 72, 73.
HALLEY. Benoni 19, 28, 84, 88; Mary

88.
HALLINGE. Ann 22, 23,69;
 Aron-36;Benjamin 23,36,
 69, Elizabeth 17, 18; John
 17,36,37,77,78; Reubin 16,17,
 32; Robert 17,36; William
 49,69.
HAMILTON. George 6, 85; James 43,
 55, 56, 77, 83, 87, 97, 102.
HAMPTON. Anthoney 23, 24; Henry
 33; Jeremiah 15; John 92.
HARLE. John 2, 19; William 19, 20, 36,
 37, 41, 81, 82.
HARRIS. Elizabeth 36.
HARRISON. Capt. 86.
HART. Daniel 85; Dr. 29..
HARTLEY. John 65.
HENDERSON. John 81.
HENSON. George 85.
HEREFORD. Jane 30; John 29, 30.
HEYSEN. 66.
HIGGERSON. John 81.
HOLLIS. John 52.
HOPKINS. Mathew 6, 13.
HOUGH. John 72, 73.
HUNT. Joseph 52.
HUNTER. John 81, 102.
HURST/HURSK. John 18,19, 20, 27,
 40; Sarah 40.
HUTCHISON. Andrew 5; John 19.
INDIAN. Tom (WADE) 44.
JAMES. Daniel 18, 19, 104.
JANNEY. Amos 72; Jane 72; Mary 72,
 73; William 62.
JARVIS. 86; The Smith 1, James 3, 4,
 28, 29, 35, 87; John 85.
JENINGS/JENNINGS. Henry 70, Edmund 98.
JENKINS. Ezll. 76; James 57, 58, 76;
 John 19, 76; Samuel 19, 75, 76;
 Jeremiah 5, 6, 14; Job 76; John
 14; Mary 75, 76, 77; William 3,
 4, 75, 76, 77, 93, 95.
JOHNSON. George 85; Samuel 105;
 Robert 85.
JONES. David 33, 34, 80, 83, 84, 88;
 Elesand 86; Lewis 88.
KING. John 15, 16, 98; Joseph 52;
 Robert 4, 5, 85.
KITCHEN. John 25, 26, 27; William 25,
 26, 84.
LASSWELL. Jacob 23, 24; John 32, 33;
 Margret 23, 24.
LAY. Abraham 82.
LEE. Richard 84.
LEWIS. Stephen 93; Thomas 43, 68, 85,
 99; Vincent 15, 48.
LINDSEY/LINCEY. Robert 5,29,101,

102.

LINTON. Moses 29, 35.

LITTLEJOHN. Silas 35.

LITTLETON. Charles 37; John 37, 38,
42, 99; Sarah 37, 38, 39, 86, 87;
Solomon 37; William 37, 38.

LOE. John 40.

LOUNDS. Chris. 84.

LUCAS. Jacob 90, 98; John 19, 20, 57,
58; Sarah 90, 91.

LYRLEYS. James 84.

MANLEY. John 43, 88, 99.

MARSHALL. Thomas 84, 85.

MARTIN. Nicholas 34, 35.

MASON. Ann 6, 29; Charles 16, 40;
Thomas 87.

MASSEY. Henry 85.

MATHEWS. Patrick 2.

MAYBE. William 18.

McCARTY. 30, 87; Ann 58, 59; Daniel
58, 59, 86; Denis 58, 59; Major
58; Mrs. 59; Sarah 18, 58, 59;
Thaddeus 59.

McDOWELL. Mary 69.

McELAIN. Cornelus 94.

McGAR. Owen 11,36;

McGEACH. Joseph 68.

McMILLION. Stephen 106

MEHONEY. William 5.

MERIWETHER. William 103.

MIDDLETON. John 33.

MILLS. Daniel 39; Robert 13.

MINOR. John 6, 16, 19, 40, 63.

MIRES. John 108

MITCHELL Elias 49, Hugh 28, 35.

MORE. (MOORE) Michl. 18; William
14, 92.

MORRIS/MORS Ebenezer 29;.
Thomas 6.

MOSLEY. Ann 52.

MOSS. 29; John 85, 98.

MOXLEY. Daniel 53; Donald 52; James
53; Jane 53; Samuel 67; Thomas
56; William 53, 67.

MURPHEY (MURPHY). John 13, 83.

MURREY. James 70.

MUSGROVE. Culvert 52; Edward 51,
52, 53; John 51, 52, 53, 67; Mary
52; Margret 52; William 52.

MUSKILL. John 96.

NEAL (NEALE) 29; Charles 4, 106,
107; Edward 1; Lewis 85; Lydia
58, 64, 65.

NEGROES. (OMOHUNDRA)
Bridget 9, Dick 9, Bess 15,Sam
16,
(PEARSON) Joe 26;

(OKEAN) Jack 40, 49;Gawah/
(Gawash) 40,49; Rachel
40,49;
(WADE) Harry 43; Gabriel 43, Moll
43, 44; Sue and child Charles 43;
Lidia 43; Jane 44; Lucy 44; Tary 44;
Murreah 44; Peter 44; Dick
(MUSGROVE) Dick 52; Tom 52;
George 52; Hannah 52; Judy 52;
(McCARTHY) Thad & child George
58,Sam, Rodham. Sawry, Jack,
Stafford, Alice, Hannah,
Maria, Sarah, Drew, Miney, Judy,
Nancy, Bob, George, Willoby, Fredrick
59; Lettice,
Phil, Will 59; Sengo, Margaret, Jack,
Sabrina, Youmg, Songo, Joan, Mary,
Young Sabrina-59;
Peter, Mullato Peter, Black Peter,
Bess Fire, Winny, Thad, Mol, Maurer,
Duke, King 59; London, Sam,Lucy,
Beck, Maria, Bess, George 59;
(BARRY) Dublin 91, Hannah 91;
Casar 92, Harry 92, George 92,
Mingo 92, Bess 92, Balenda 92;
(TAYLOR) Bess 93.

NELSON. Secretary 29.

NOLAND. Philip 22, 23, 32, 49, 78.

NORTH. John 59, 60, 72.

NORWOOD. John 74.

OKEAN. Henry 40, 41, 49, 50; Jenny
40, 41, 50; Richard 40.

OMOHUNDRA. Ann 9, 10; Elizabeth 9,
10, 11; Jane 9, 10; Richard 9, 10,
14 15, 47, 48; Sarah 9, 10; William
10.

ONEAL. (ONEALE) Charles 65.

OSBORN. Ann 16, 78; Capt. 71, 85;
Richard 2, 7, 18, 43, 61, 68, 78,
79, 84, 86, 87, 88; Robert 15, 16,
78.

OWSLEY. Thomas 91.

PAGAN. John 1, 2, 12, 13, 15, 16, 18,
70, 71, 98, 102, 107.

PARISHES. Truro 7, 36, 37, 40, 53, 75,
77, 81, 91.

PARSONS. William 53.

PAYNE. 87; John 2; William 1, 15, 16,
29, 35, 38, 39, 47, 63, 74, 75, 95,
97, 105.

PEAKE. John 74; William 7.

PEARSON. Simon 22, 26, 27, 65, 66;
Thomas 6, 15, 18.

PEIRCE. Thomas 44.

PENSILVANIA, Lancaster County 40.

PENSON/PINSON. Joseph 9, 10, 11;
Mary 9; Richard Omohundra 9;

112

www.ingramcontent.com/pod-product-compliance
Lightning Source LLC
Chambersburg PA
CBHW080337270326
41927CB00014B/3258